THE LORD'S SUPPER

IT'S NOT WHAT YOU THINK

Anthony bud weishaar

Dedication

I would like to dedicate this book to my first mentors in Christ from the little town of Mission Hills California, just a couple of miles north-east of Lompoc, CA., and just a mile or two from the largest mission in California, the La Purisima Mission. I mention the location because I'm not originally from that area, but it became, along with the entire central coast area, one of my absolute favorite places on God's green earth and I've been to a lot of places throughout the US and abroad.

Moreover, it was the people of the two local churches of Christ there, one in Mission Hills the other in Lompoc on O Street, that were instrumental in my life. With an honorable mention to the church of Christ on Clark Ave., and also on Foster Rd. in nearby Santa Maria.

My primary mentors were Lynn Swenson and his wife Sue, along with Dave Swain and his wife Mona. Their love, patience, goodness and kindness toward me was immeasurable. Not to mention their hospitality which kept me well fed and entertained. Along with them were Gordon and Kathy Johnson and Mark and Mary Tobin and their respective families, all of whom played key roles in my coming to Christ and remaining with the Lord through some very challenging times. And of course, many thanks to the incredible Huie family.

Beyond these I owe a debt of gratitude to my brothers Dane and Bret Bengard with whom I hammered out a lot of my understanding. Also, to Randy Hohf with whom I scaled the heights of Mt. Whitney and Mt. Rainer, and who introduced me to John Mark Hick's book, "Come to the Table" (who I met a few years later at the Pepperdine college lectures), both were instrumental in retooling my mind and spirit. Finally, muchas gracias to my friend and brother Cecilio Gonzales with whom I shared many a table in San Diego and walked out the practical aspects of living by the life of Christ, along with many other brothers and sisters with whom I shared body life in the ekklesia there and also now

A. Bud Weishaar......May 2023

Table of Contents

Introduction

One of the aspects we are trying to draw attention to in this book on the Lord's supper is the importance of the social dimension of the supper.

To this very day we are trying to unravel and disentangle from centuries of erroneous teachings that have stifled our fellowship, halted our spiritual maturity, codified and cauterized our thinking into one of two categories:

1. The medieval practice of the Roman Catholic "Mass" that changes the bread and wine into the literal flesh and blood of Jesus Christ through the process of "transubstantiation" at the "altar table."
2. The Reformation practice of a "worship service" during which a silent, somber ten-minute "memorial supper" is conducted from a "symbolic table" in memory of the Lord Jesus.

In the course of our study, we'll notice that by definition a "supper" is not a snack. And that there is no mention of "transubstantiation" in the New Testament writings, nor is there ever a "Mass" conducted by Jesus, his Apostles, by Paul or any of their fellow church workers, not to mention a future ordained set of priests who perform a "Mass."

Obviously stating this in the introduction may well prompt you to drop this book in the circular file. Or you may continue to read with a curious spirit. Either way, one thing will become obvious, we are equal opportunity offenders. Not intentionally, we simply realize the nature of personal religious convictions and most "Christians" are easily offended when theirs are called into question much less contradicted (even by Scripture).

However, if you are questioning you're religious beliefs and convictions, or with what your church teaches and practices, or you've become discontented with life, even disappointed with God, whatever it may be, I give you this guarantee; there is no greater pursuit in life you can make than to know and draw ever closer to Jesus Christ, and in your relationship to other believers who are also seeking a deeper, closer relationship with the Lord, because he is the only one who can set things right, and usher you into the presence of the Father, His Father and yours.

But just saying that doesn't mean it's going to be easy, as every relationship takes effort.

So, if you are comfortable with where you're at in your relationship to God, doing the "worship service" with the "chip & sip" Lord's supper, or sitting through the "Mass" with its ritual "transubstantiation" ceremony, reading this will be little more than an academic exercise. You may learn something, but will it change anything?

All we are offering is a fresh look at the Lord Jesus Christ, who is as near to you as your own breath, Romans 10:8-10.

Every Table is a Teaching Table

A huge chuck of Jesus' ministry revolved around the table, eating and drinking with people in face-2-face fellowship, forging personal relationships while calling *"whosoever will"* to participate in the Kingdom of God.

In fact, food was a major reference point in the ministry of Jesus even when he wasn't actually eating, *"I have food to eat of which you do not know"* (Jn. 4:32-38).

It has been said; "Practice ought to be laid hold of before theory."[1] That is, Scripture's ought to be walked out in experience first, and knowledge second. In reality it's a parallel process, like riding a tandem bicycle. Today we have it completely flipped; we have a theory but never put it into a living practice. Which is to say, we never leave the class-room for the laboratory; we never break the huddle to actually run the play.

From the opening curtain of Jesus' birth in a manger in Bethlehem[2] where he was laid in a food trough from which animals ate, to the closing scene of the "last supper" in Jerusalem[3] where Jesus enjoyed his last meal with friends before His crucifixion and resurrection, He ate continuously, both physically and spiritually.

---

[1] From the writings of the late 1600's of Michael Molinos.

[2] Bethlehem means, "House of Bread."

[3] Jerusalem means, "Mountain Fortress of God, Stronghold." See Isaiah 2:2, f.

3

Luke records some of the most prominent teaching tables Jesus took part in during His ministry:

> ➢ Luke 5, Jesus eats with tax collectors and "sinners" in the home of Levi,[4] and he teaches the people.
> ➢ Luke 7, Jesus eats in the home of Simon the Pharisee and his feet are washed with tears and anointed with perfume, and he teaches the people.
> ➢ Luke 9, Jesus feeds five-thousand on a hill side, and he teaches the people.
> ➢ Luke 10, Jesus eats in the home of Mary and Martha and he teaches the disciples.
> ➢ Luke 11, Jesus eats lunch with some Pharisees and lawyers and teaches against them for their legalistic, self-righteous attitudes, and he teaches the people.
> ➢ Luke 14, Jesus eats bread with a leading Pharisee and lawyers on the Sabbath, and he heals and teaches the people. A lot!
> ➢ Luke 19, Jesus eats dinner with Zacchaeus, and he teaches the people.
> ➢ Luke 22, Jesus eats the last supper with his disciples (which is the first of many to follow), and he teaches them.

➢ Luke 24, now risen, Jesus eats with two disciples from Emmaus, and again later that same evening he eats with the disciples in Jerusalem and teaches them. A you can see, every table Jesus took part in was a functional

---

[4] Levi is Matthew the apostle who was a tax collector, as is Zacchaeus, Lk. 19.

teaching table. We conclude; Table time is a time to teach.

Throughout the Gospels Jesus shared many tables with all kinds of people, from Jerusalem to Galilee, from hill sides to dining halls, from the strait laced self-righteous Jewish Pharisees to the despised Jewish tax collectors, loose living women, and despised Samaritans, yet one thing all Jews shared in common, as a matter of Mosaic heritage, was eating celebratory meals together. Meals like the Passover coupled with the feast of Unleavened Bread in particular was a festive occasion that celebrated Israels freedom from Egyptian bondage by the mighty hand of God. These meals were eaten at home with the entire family, and marked by joy.

For centuries Israel enjoyed these dinning events together around the family dinner table, including every Sabbath day.[5]

But then something very strange happened on the day of Pentecost,[6] some three-thousand Jews were converted to Christ, but instead of eating a joyful celebratory meal that recalled Jesus' triumph over death and their new found freedom in Him, they are now being taught to sit in utter silence as they eat a morsel of unleavened bread and a sip of wine as the "Lord's Supper." This while

---

5 Ironically, one of the two rooms of the tabernacle was a dining room of sorts. The Holy Place with the Table of Showbread with twelve loaves of unleavened bread that the priests ate every Sabbath.

[6] See, Acts 2 for this event, especially the eating *"form house to house"* that followed.

setting in pews, front-to-back with a symbolic table up front with the words; *"Do this in remembrance of Me"*[7] engraved on it. Does this seem likely to you?

It's either that, or watch a Mass be performed by one of the apostles, wherein "transubstantiation" is performed that changes the unleavened bread and wine into the literal body and blood of Jesus and eat a little wafer-host of tasteless bread as Romanism teaches. Which seems even less likely.

Nevertheless, those are our two options based upon where we are today.

In both cases they are done in a controlled somber atmosphere, in utter silence without any semblance of a meal being eaten, much less in a joyful and open face-to-face fellowship.

Neither of these two options match the Scriptures which shows that the fulfillment is always greater than what it forecasted; the reality is greater than the shadow; the anti-type greater than the type; the new is greater than the old. This is nowhere better illustrated than the lamb of the Passover as fulfilled in Jesus Christ, the Lamb of God.

In Luke's account of the last supper a dispute broke out among the disciple about who was greatest among them. Jesus had already addressed this matter once before,[8]

_____

[7] See, Luke 22:19.
[8] See, Matt. 20:20-28; Mk. 10:35-45 (see also, Matt. 23:1-12; 18:1-6).

but obviously it didn't stick. So again, He addresses it but with greater attention, and an added dimension concerning servant leadership, which involves being a table waiter;

"You are those who have stood by Me in my trials; and just as the Father has granted Me a kingdom, I grant you that you may eat and drink at My table in My Kingdom, and you will sit on thrones judging the twelve tribes of Israel" (Luke 22:28-30, et., al.).

The very first "leadership" roles that appeared in the church in Jerusalem (outside of Apostles) are, you guessed it; "table waiters." Acts 6 tells us that the church in Jerusalem selected seven spirit filled men to wait tables. Servant leadership has always been and still is God's way.

In the ekklesia of Christ, no one graduates with honors without serving others as Jesus Himself did, who set the example by washing their feet; *"If I then, the Lord and the Teacher washed your feet, you also ought to wash one another's feet. For I gave you an example that you also should do as I did to you" (John 13:14-15).*

Leadership serves, even to the point of death. That is the point of the cross.

"To the hungry soul, every bitter thing is sweet" (Prov. 27:7b).

The Lord's Supper; It's not what you think.

(From theology to experience; Recovering the lost history of the covenant family meal)

Chapter 1

Acts 2—The Lord's Supper

(A general discussion on the Lord's Supper from Acts 2)[9]

"An old error is always

more popular than

a new truth."

--German proverb

Many churches (especially Churches of Christ[10]) propose that the Lord's supper be made more meaningful because of criticism that the "worship services are cold and

---

[9] Biblical passages are cited form the New American Standard, unless otherwise noted.

[10] "The Lord's Supper" (Do this in remembrance of Me), a workbook, by Dick Blackford, 2005.

meaningless."[11] This criticism implies that for some churches their time together is not very meaningful or spiritually encouraging. Routine has a way of doing that. But I would suggest that simply lengthening the time spent in silence preparing to eat the Lord's supper will not make it less cold or more meaningful.

Typically, the supper only lasts a very short time in the course of the worship service, yet appears to be one of the primary reasons for coming together on the first day of the week, and plays a central role in the gathering of believers as witnessed in Acts 2, Acts 20 and I Corinthians 11.

The churches written about in the New Testament didn't gather on the first day of the week to simply conduct a "worship service." To be blunt, the "worship service" was invented by man, introduced by the Roman Catholic Church in the early ages, and adopted by the Reformers in the Middle Ages, and has filtered down to us in the modern Church age.[12]

In Churches of Christ (with which I am most familiar and with whom the author quoted above, identifies), the worship service revolves around the-Five-Acts-of-Worship, via Acts 2:42:

1. The Apostles teaching (evangelism in the preaching and Bible classes)

---

[11] Ibid, chapter 1, Introduction, and Pg. 58.
[12] "Church History in plain language," Bruce Shelley, 2nd ed, 1995; "Christianity, the first three thousand years," Diarmaid MacCulloch, 2009.

2. Fellowship (which includes giving of your means)
3. The Breaking of Bread (interpreted as the traditional Lord's supper)
4. Prayer, and singing* (*though not mentioned is considered the 5th act of worship)

Some go so far as to say, if a "worship service" does not include all five of these acts of worship it's not really a biblical worship service, and perhaps you've sinned.

The "worship service" they say, consists of preaching, giving (i.e., fellowship), the Lord's supper, prayer and singing. Virtually all modern denominations (not just churches of Christ) follow this format with very little deviation.[13] Churches of Christ hold to this pattern very strongly, yet there is not one single example of such a Sunday meeting in all the New Testament that follows this procedure, and Acts 2:42 is not prescriptive, it is merely descriptive of what the Jerusalem church did but in no intended particular order, much less in a formal manner.

Furthermore, there is no "necessary inference" for this procedure, much less a "direct command" (both of which are used to establish biblical authority for a thing to be done among cocer's[14]), or any "approved apostolic examples," also part of establishing biblical authority.[15]

---

[13] "The Encyclopedia of the Stone-Campbell Movement," editors, 2004, Eerdmans Pub. Co.

[14] "Cocer's" is short for Church of Christ hereafter.

[15] Typically, the "worship service" is explained as an expedient. Meaning, in order to get through the five acts of worship, the

So why do denominations and coc's cling so tenaciously to the Sunday "worship service" for which there is no biblical president? In a word ~" tradition."

We make many assumptions about what the Scriptures teach because of the traditions we've inherited and looking through the prism of modern church practices. So, in spite of what God's word reveals; "we practice what we believe and we believe what we practice." And this is certainly the case when it comes to the Lord's supper but the bigger problem is the concept of a "worship service." Because every "act of worship" is fitted into the worship service.

If we ask ourselves, was Luke prescribing a procedure to be followed in every Sunday worship service when he wrote Acts 2? Or was he simply recording what the believers continually devoted themselves to on a day-by-day basis as verse 42 say's, "*day by day continuing with* ***one mind...***". We conclude its option number 2, and descriptive.

But we've turned this into a very formal every Sunday worship service, and prescriptive.

So, we ask, "Continually devoted to what!?" A routine Sunday worship service that repeats the 5-acts of worship? No, they were devoted to simply knowing the Lord Jesus Christ, "*with one mind*" (v.46). And that did not follow a standardized "worship service," their

---

clergy/leaders regulate the time devoted to each act. Which relegates the Lord's day to only an hour or two, not all day.

meetings were not timed, or followed a set order, there was no church building, they met from house to house and for a time under Solomon's portico in the temple precincts, Acts 3:11; 4:12. All of their meetings appear to be quite spontaneous and without a set order, such as is practiced today.

Discipleship in Action

Are we saying there was not worship? Or teaching? Or giving? Breaking bread and prayer? Singing? Fasting? Discipline? Baptizing? Encouraging, etc, etc? No, all that was taking place, but free of formality, it was quite natural, spontaneous and organic, as opposed to a set, formal, institutionalized worship service. All of it is part and parcel of *learning* Jesus Christ (Matthew 11:28-30; Ephesians 4:20, 23).

All we are saying is that you cannot find a "worship service" where a church is following the five acts of worship (in part or in whole) in the New Testament writings in any set order such as is practiced today by virtually every Christian denomination.

Now we ask our traditional Lord's supper brethren, when the disciples were meeting at Solomon's portico at the temple were they sharing the Lord's Supper there together on the first day of the week?

If so, were they passing the trays around with little pieces of unleavened bread? And then trays with the little cuplets of the fruit of the vine? All while setting in stone cold silence contemplating their sins and meditating on the Lord Jesus nailed to the cross? For three thousand people that would have taken awhile. Did that make it more meaningful?

Or did they only eat the Lord's supper from house to house on the first day of the week, with smaller groups of believers? The traditional Lord's supper, consisting of a small piece of unleavened bread and a sip of the fruit of the vine, again while setting in silence contemplating their Lord upon the cross for their sins?

We may also ask, why does Luke bother to tell us at all of the eating habits of the Jerusalem believers who were doing this at the temple (?), and from house to house; *"taking their meals together with gladness and sincerity of heart"* (?), unless these meals were spiritual, or creating a spiritual connection among these believers and with the Lord? But most cocer's reject this idea that a meal eaten at home (a social meal) has any spiritual meaning at all. To quote brother Blackford; "There is nothing inherently spiritual about a common meal...".[16] If so, then what Luke tells us about their "common meals" is quite pointless as there was nothing spiritual about them and were merely secular.

At this point we would like to ask our traditional Lord's supper brethren two questions:

1. When you eat a regular meal do you first pray, thanking God for your food and asking him to

---

[16] Ibid, pg. 59, under "Other Radical Admissions."

bless it to the nourishment of your body? Does this make it spiritual?

2. When Jesus reclined at the table to eat with the two disciples from Emmaus, we read, "*he took the bread and blessed it, and breaking it, he began giving it to them...*", was this; a). a common meal? b). a spiritual meal? c). both?[17]

(Okay, that was more than two questions, but who's counting?)

Additionally, acts 2:47 says they did all this eating together while "*praising God and having favor with all the people.*" How does eating common meals together result in *praising God* so as to curry favor with all the people so that the *Lord adds* to their number daily those being *saved*?? Unless this eating together is actually a spiritual event that displays the Lord Jesus among the community of believers.

All this eating and active praising of God just does not match the practice of today's traditional Lord's supper brethren, who sit in silence and even sing a very somber song to put them in the mood to remember the dying Lord Jesus on the cross, and their sin which put him there in order to eat a single chip of unleavened bread and a single sip of wine. Much less does it match the "*house to house*" pattern of verse 47.

It is commonly taught in the coc's that Acts 2:42, "*the breaking of bread*" is not the same "*breaking bread*" of

---

[17] See Luke 24:30.

verse 46, even though it is the same Greek wording, except for the definite article *"the"* in v.42. This, they say, distinguishes it as the Lord's supper, whereas v.46, just two sentences later, is referring to an ordinary meal.

So even though Luke uses the same wording, we're supposed to know one refers to the Lord's supper and the other does not, based upon his use of the definite article (?). This is not at all clear, especially since he did not use the definite article in Acts 20:7, we read;

*"On the first day of the week, when we were gathered to **break bread**, Paul began talking to them, intending to leave the next day, and he prolonged his message until midnight."* (This they say **is** the Lord's supper, yet the definite article is not used).

But just two sentences later, verse 11, we read;

> *"When he had gone back up and had broken **the bread** and eaten, he talked with them a long while until daybreak, and he left."*

Now they say this is <u>not</u> the Lord's supper because it is after the midnight hour, making it Monday (and the Lord's supper is only eaten on Sunday), even though the definite article precedes *"the bread."* They exact opposite of v.7, and Acts 2:42 and 46! Confused? You're not alone.

Going back to Acts 2:42 and *"the breaking of bread"* in the context of teaching, fellowship and prayer. I'm sure we all agree this phrase is referring to the Lord's supper but not because of the definite article, it has nothing to do with it. Just like Acts 20:7 is referring to the Lord's supper, but not because it lacks the definite article. And none of what Luke writes in Acts 2:42 through 47 establishes a set worship service, with the so-called 5-acts of worship, and if the 5-acts are not followed, and performed as some contend, each Lord's Day, well you might as well of stayed home! Which would be pretty hard to do, seeing that the church met in their homes.[18]

Luke is simply writing a narrative of events to Theophilus[19] without doctrine being the issue, or establishing a doctrine concerning a worship service and what the Lord's supper consists of, or how it is to be eaten (except communally) and where.[20]

Again, the phrase is the same with or without the definite article and means the exact same thing in both Acts 2:42, 46 and Acts 20; "breaking bread" means to eat a meal. And it doesn't matter if it is a regular meal or the Lord's supper.

If we really want meaningful, and dare I say *radical change* to take place, in and among the Lord's people so that we may be a truly transformed people, the first

---

[18] Not only does the biblical record show the church met in their homes, the historical record also shows this up until early in the 4th century with the advent of the emperor Constantine.

[19] See Acts 1:1, the first account was the Gospel of Luke.

[20] The phrase "breaking bread" or "the breaking of the bread" was and still is a common saying without any religious or spiritual connotations (except for the context), simply means to "eat a meal." Analogous to our saying; "let's grab a bite to eat."

step is to move outside the institutional church system and into a real and living relationship with one another. Like a real family would experience at home with mom, dad, brothers and sisters.

Real change has never happened in an established, institutional church system, be it the Roman Catholic Church, Greek Orthodox, Lutheran Church, Presbyterian Church, Methodist Church, Church of Christ, Christian Church, Baptist Church, Assemblies of God, a Synagogue or any other institutional Church or Assembly. Real change has only ever taken place when people dared to step outside the accepted institutional system.

Change (but not for the sake of change) has only ever taken place by an individual or two, sometimes three who dared to step outside the prefabed system of acceptable Church gatherings because *"their eyes were opened"* (Lk. 24:31), their *"hearts burning within them"* (v.32), and they cannot sit still any more than a perpetual motion machine. Seven miles or no seven miles, the dark of night or no dark of night, these two-disciple hot-footed it back to Jerusalem for the sake of the Lord Jesus for he *"has really risen!!"* (v.34). And their hearts burning desire was to share that good news with the other disciples right now!

Pray the Lord raises up more disciple like these two from Emmaus.

Because change is unlikely to occur within the walled confines of the modern organized institutional Church.[21]

STEP OUT!!!

---

[21] The ekklesia is not based on organization. The ekklesia is a living organism, and in the body of Christ there are no vestigial organs.

Chapter 2
I Corinthians 11—The Lord's Supper

(A general discussion on the Lord's Supper from I Corinthians 10-11)

"It is easier to believe a lie one has heard

a thousand times than to believe a fact

one has never heard before."

--author unknown

Coming out of Catholicism, it took me several months to read, study and pray for better understanding and enlightenment concerning God's ways in some very basic matters. I started with passages like, *"Do not call anyone on earth your father; for one is your Father, He who is in heaven"* (Matt. 23:9). This is in the context of the Jewish leaders taking honorary titles to themselves and lording over the people of God.

Seeing that this was directly contrary to what I had been taught in Catholicism, and having never read a Bible before—ever, I began to wonder what else was in that book.

From there I began to explore the subject of baptism and quickly discovered two things:

1. Faith was a prerequisite to baptism.
2. Only believing adults who could express their faith in Christ while repenting of sins were baptized.

There are a number of biblical passages that appealed to me[22] and a number of themes that continually came up. One of those themes is found in I Corinthians 10:1-2, we read:

"For I do not want you to be unaware, brethren, that our fathers were all under the cloud and they all passed through the sea; and they all were baptized into Moses in the cloud and in the sea..."

This occurred in Exodus 14, where God lead His people out of Egyptian captivity by His servant Moses. This included the entire nation of Israel, men, women and children of all ages, including infants in that great horde of people, an entire nation!

Even though the entire nation was baptized into Moses (a type of Christ), all that first generation of Israel, from 20 years of age and upward died in the wilderness due to their disobedience and distrust of God to lead them into the land of Canaan. Only Joshua and Caleb of that first generation, who expressed their faith and

---

[22] See Mark 16:16-17; Matt. 20:18-20; and John the Baptists' baptizing, Mark 1:4-8, who also baptized Jesus himself, vv. 9-10; Luke 3:21-22; *"all the people were being baptized"* who could repent of sins. See also Acts 2:37-38; Romans 6. All through Acts I kept asking: "Where are infant children explicitly being baptized?"

trust in God were allowed to enter the Promised Land of Canaan along with all of that second generation of Israel of 19 years of age and younger.[23] This is all recorded in Numbers chapters 13 and 14.[24]

Why was that younger generation allowed to enter? Because God did not hold them responsible, or accountable for their parent's sin of rebellion. Read and compare the contexts of Numbers 14:31 and Deuteronomy 1:39 in order;

Before: "*As for your children that you said would be taken as plunder, I will bring them in to enjoy the land you have rejected."*

After: "*And the little ones that you said would be taken captive, your children who do not yet know good from bad—they will enter the land. I will give it to them and they will take possession of it."*

So, we see the larger context of the story of these two generations between Numbers and Deuteronomy, and that 2nd generation that has now grown up, having reached the age of accountability, they will now take

---

[23] Others of the Levitical tribe above the age of 20, also entered the "Promise Land." See, Joshua 14:1; 24:7; Judges 2:7. Aaron's sons Eleazar & Ithamar were anointed at Mt. Sinai, see Lev. 8; 10:6-7, at the age of 25, when they could serve in the tent of meeting.

[24] See also Ezekiel 18, the entire chapter say's the soul that sins shall die (v.20). Children do not inherit the sins of their parents nor held accountable for their forefathers' sins, hence no "original sin" doctrine. Each is responsible for himself or herself before God Almighty.

responsibility for themselves to God and thus are baptized into Joshua (who assumes leadership after Moses, Deut. 34:9, and is also a type of Christ) in the Jordan River as recorded in Joshua chapter 3. Hence, their first baptism didn't count, necessitating their second baptism.

Another prominent theme in the Old Testament of coming through water as a type of baptism is seen in the flood of Noah, recorded in Genesis 7 and 8, and mentioned by Peter:

"...the patience of God kept waiting in the days of Noah, during the construction of the ark, in which a few, that is, eight persons, were brought safely through the water. Corresponding to that, baptism now saves you—not the removal of dirt from the flesh, but an appeal to God for a good conscience—through the resurrection of Jesus Christ..." (I Peter 3:20-21).

Do you see how God uses this deliverance through water as a theme of death, burial and resurrection? First the Red Sea, then the Jordan River, and in the flood of Noah. All three represent a type of baptism into death followed by a resurrection unto new life.

Soon I discovered even more themes of watery baptisms into death; the story of Jonah in the belly of the whale; Naaman the leper baptized in the Jordan River; Elisha recovering the lost axe head in the Jordan River (see in order Jonah 1, 2; II Kings 5; II Kings 6).

All of this was very new and very exciting to me, not to mention a little scary as it was challenging my previous beliefs in my Catholic upbringing. But the more I read, studied and prayed about all of this the clearer it became to me.[25]

Crisis events like these, usually coupled with one or two other life events is how God gets our attention. To paraphrase C.S. Lewis; "Pain is God's megaphone to a deaf world." And sadly, some of those reside in the church, just as they did in Israel.

Among other things that I learned about baptism, besides the prerequisite of faith, repentance, and adults being baptized, was the "mode" along with the very definition of the word. And this is the important matter.

1st: I kept seeing that it was a complete submersion of one's entire body, as Romans 6:3-5 describes, as John the Baptist practiced, and as the Old Testament types revealed.

2nd: The Greek word for baptism is "baptizo", a verb that literally means to immerse, and never does it mean sprinkle or pour. It only ever means one thing; immerse or submerge.

---

[25] Hebrews 6:1-2 tells us, among other things, that baptism is a matter of elementary teaching, along with repentance, faith in God, laying on of hands, resurrection and eternal judgment. All of which are matters for an adult, as opposed to a child or an infant.

There are other Greek words for "sprinkle" and "pour" but they are never used in association with a believer's baptism.[26]

Convinced of this truth and of my own volition, I took the plunge and was baptized into Christ for the remission of my sins at the age of twenty-two.

As I learned Christ the more adjustments I made to my walk. And those adjustments have been as numerous as the sands of the sea and many painful. And still occurring to this very day.

**One of those adjustments concerned the Lord's supper. Eventually I learned there were others, including in the Churches of Christ, that understood the Lord's supper to actually be a full meal, around a real actual table in the homes of fellow believers. This too was exciting and scary. They saw the Lord's supper as the fulfillment of the Jewish Passover feast. And for good reason as I found out.[27]

But just like I defended my Catholic faith at first, I also defended my traditional understanding and practice of

---

[26] For *sprinkle* see, Leviticus chapters 1-5 for the many times it is used; Hebrews chapters 9-10; I Peter 1:2. For *pour* see, Leviticus chapters 2-4 of the pouring out of blood and oil; Matt. 26:7, 12; Acts 2:17-18; 10:45; Revelation 16:2-17.
[27] "Come to the Table", John Mark Hicks, 2008; "A meal with Jesus" by Tim Chester, 2011; "Making a meal of it", by Ben Witherington III, 2007; "From tablet to table," Leonard Sweet, 2014; and numerous other books, documents, studies, discussions, conferences and internet sites on this topic.

the Lord's supper at first. Because-"I believed what I practiced, and I practice what I believe."

One of the issues that kept coming up, like the word "baptizo" and it's literal meaning (and coc's are sticklers for literal word meanings), the word "supper" kept coming up. The Greek word is "deipnon" and is used in a number of places, especially in I Corinthian 11, verses 20-21 and 25, which is the same wording as Luke's version[28] of the "last supper" that Jesus shared with his disciples on the night he was betrayed.

There were other Greek words available to the New Testament writers if they wanted to indicate something less than a full meal. But they didn't, writers of the New Testament consistently used this word "deipnon" in association with the Lord's supper, which by definition is nothing less than a full meal, commonly eaten in the evening.

The word "supper" (Gk. deipnon), means to eat a full meal and implies food enough to satisfy hunger. The Lord's supper menu included unleavened bread and fruit of the vine (or wine), but was not limited to just the unleavened bread and drink any more than the Passover was limited to just the unleavened bread and wine. If the Lord's supper were limited to just unleavened bread and fruit of the vine, it never would have been called a "supper." This is in fact why some at Corinth were eating and drinking their fill while others went hungry, vv.20-21.

---

[28] See Luke 22:20, "in the same way he took the cup after supper...".

This is why some have wisecracked it as "the Lord's snack" or "the chip and sip" in referring to the supper as commonly practiced today.

The traditional way of eating the Lord's supper simply does not fit the biblical narrative or the meaning of the word "*supper*" any more than sprinkling fits the narrative or the meaning of the word "*baptism.*"

So, I ask my traditional brethren; **If it's not a supper, by definition, what is it?**

We may also as ask our baby baptizing brethren; **If baptism is not by immersion, is it really a baptism?**

One thing I think we can all agree upon, the Lord's supper should certainly include the unleavened bread and the fruit of the vine, otherwise it's little more than a baptism by sprinkling.[29]

A common question we're often asked concerning the supper being a full meal is;

"How much food do I have to eat?"

This is mostly "a got ya question" geared toward derailing the conversation in favor of the traditional "chip & sip."

Our response is; "How much water do we need to be fully immersed, as the word Greek word *baptizo* is defined?"

---

[29] Unless you hold the view of "transubstantiation," which will be addressed in a following chapter.

Consistent with that, John 3:23, actually tells us that John the Baptist "was baptizing in Aenon near Salim, because there was much water there...".

So, to be baptize you need enough water to be fully immersed, and in eating the supper you need enough food to be fully satisfied. Baptism is more than a sprinkling, and the supper is more than a chip and sip. And it is entirely possible to have enough water to immerse[30] and enough food to be satisfied.

And for those who have come to see the supper is not limited to just bread and wine also see that baptism is more than just sprinkling. They will have nothing less than the Lord's highest; a complete bodily immersion in the Lord, and a complete Lord's supper that will satisfy their appetite, both spiritually and physically. Eating meals together is a socially binding activity in every culture. The ekklesia too has a culture and it is the fulfilled culture of the Israelite people with whom God started and is now continuing in the Christian community (Galatians 6:16).

Revealing Meals

One of the aspects of eating the Lord's supper together is to reveal the Lord among us. This was precisely what happened at the "last supper" with Judas and exactly the problem that was going on in Corinth.

---

[30] See, Acts 8:38-39.

The fact, that I Corinthians 11:18, tells us that the church was gathered together to eat the Lord's supper (v.20), but some ended up eating their own individual suppers (v.21), not only sets the context but reveals the problem at the same time.

Again, the problem with Judas (at the last supper) was that he ended up pursuing his own interests right in the midst of that covenant meal with the Lord Jesus and the other disciples.[31] He could have said no to his own interests, but of course he didn't.[32] We agree with the sentiment of Dietrich Bonhoeffer who said Judas Iscariot "will always be a dark riddle and an awful warning."[33] Similarly, some of those in Corinth pursued their own interests right in the midst of the supper of the Lord with their brethren.

How? By eating their *"own supper first"* with a blatant disregard for the Lord and their brethren *"who have nothing"* (v.22). They too suffered for their disregard, I Cor. 11:30; *"For this reason many among you are weak, and sick, and a number asleep."*

I Corinthians shows us that the center of our meetings is Jesus Christ and when we are eating his supper together, he is revealing himself in and among us. This is explicitly stated in 14:23-26; *"When the whole church assembles together...",* which includes eating the supper

---

[31] See John 13.

[32] Satan certainly had a strong influence on Judas, yet was not forced against his own will.

[33] "The Cost of Discipleship" D. Bonhoeffer, 1949, Collier Books, MacMillan Pub. Co.

together, each part of the body of believers shares their food with everyone present and what the Lord is revealing in each member of the body. The results are two-fold:

1. The unbeliever is brought to faith, 14:23-25
2. Each believer shares his or her spiritual gift, v.26

We read;

"What is the outcome then, brethren? When you assemble, each one has a Psalm, has a teaching, has a revelation. Let all things be done for edification."

The best teacher is experience, and one thing about Christianity is that it is meant to be experienced. Every aspect of living by the indwelling life of Christ[34] is meant to be lived out *"day by day"* especially in the community of believers.

It has been rightly said; "Christianity is not a spectator sport; it is a participatory sport." Because the kingdom of God is a kingdom of Co-Ed participation.

Getting to know your brothers and sisters better (in whom the Lord Jesus dwells) is an inevitable experience of any meal and especially at the table of the Lord

---

[34] See I Cor. 15:45, Jesus is *"a life-giving Spirit"* who indwells each believer by faith so as to live by his life; eating of him, Jn. 6:57; partaking of his divine nature, I Pet. 1:4; conformed to and reflecting his image, Rom. 8:29; *"transformed into the same image"*, II Cor. 3:18; Christ formed in you, Galatians 2:20; 4:19. The ekklesia is the corporate image of Christ.

because it is intended to mediate God's covenant of peace to us and bring us together in a communal meal time. Our common-union is centered on the Lord Jesus, who is the host, who provides the food we share, and our experiences in Christ are shared at the Lord's table and throughout the meeting.

Setting the Table

In I Cor. 11, Paul takes us back to the "last supper" which was a Passover meal between Jesus and his disciples and in the midst of that meal the Lord takes bread, and says it is his body; that is, the unleavened bread represents his body, vv.23-24.[35]

Then he takes the cup *"after supper"* (v.25) and says this is my blood. That is, the drink represents his blood. So that it does not escape our notice, a *supper* (consistent with the Gk. wd. "deipnon") means a full meal, one that satisfies our appetite, and it is a spiritual meal. We point this out again only because many of our brethren ask, "Well, how much food do I have to eat?" Our answer (besides the one above); "...it depends on your level of hunger and your appetite. Just as at any supper, or meal." No one should leave the table hungry or thirsty.

For the Jewish people the Passover was a family meal, an evening supper. If you were part of a small family, you invited your neighbors to share the supper, each

_____

[35] That this is figurative speech and not literal is clearly seen from John 10:6-10; *"I am the door…"*, which is also figurative language.

according to what he or she could eat so that ideally, there were no leftovers, Exodus 12:3-4, 8, 10;

"Speak to all the congregation of Israel, saying, 'On the tenth of this month they are, each one, to take a lamb for themselves, according to the fathers' households, a lamb for each household. Now if the household is too small for a lamb, then he and his neighbor nearest to his house are to take one according to the number of persons in them; **in proportion to what each one should eat**, you are to divide the lamb ... They shall eat the flesh that same night, roasted with fire, and they shall eat it with unleavened bread and bitter herbs ... And you shall **not leave any** of it over until morning, but whatever is left of it until morning, you shall completely burn with fire."

This is the meal Jesus was sharing with his disciples at the so-called "last supper." And yes, it was a memorial supper and memorial meals are not inherently sad, somber, remorseful and funeralistic such as is the attitude of the traditional Lord's supper that is eaten in most every evangelical church today.

And if we've missed that point, we need only read verse 14 of this Exodus chapter;

"Now this day shall be a **memorial** to you, and you shall **celebrate** it as a **feast** to the Lord; throughout your *generations you are to **celebrate** it as a permanent ordinance."* [36]

This annual memorial meal was a feast and a celebration of the Hebrew people's deliverance out of the bondage of Egypt by means of the death and shed blood of the lamb, and eating the lamb **in proportion to his or her appetite**. This eating is what energized and empowered the people of Israel to flee that very night from their Egyptian captures.

Celebratory Meals

The Passover memorial meal is similar to our annual 4th of July holiday which is a celebration of America's independence from English rule. It is a celebration of our freedom, an eating holiday. Similarly, our annual Thanksgiving Day celebration is an eating holiday when we thank God for all his blessings.

The Lord's supper is no different, it is a celebratory occasion, like a home run, a touchdown, a graduation, a wedding, or a New Years celebration—all of which are marked by rejoicing! If during such an event a person were setting alone looking somber and sad, we would naturally ask, "What's wrong?" In fact, Deuteronomy 26:14 actually forbids mourning during these festive occasions.

------

[36] Compare this with Deut. 16:1-2, 10-14; II Chron. 30 and 35, remember to *"celebrate Passover."*

Jesus said, "I have earnestly desired to eat this Passover with you before I suffer", this specific annual feast celebrated by the Hebrew people is fulfilled in Jesus as "the Lamb of God"[37] sacrificed on the cross, of which the altar was a symbol, just as the lamb was a symbol of Christ himself. Continuing, "for I say to you, I shall never again eat it until it is fulfilled in the kingdom of God."[38] This meal with Jesus is the only one that continues of all the festive meals God inaugurated with His people Israel, albeit it now celebrates our deliverance in Christ from the bondage of "the spiritual forces of wickedness in heavenly places" (Eph. 6:12). And he continues to eat with us now that it has been fulfilled in the kingdom of God.

Side Dish

God gave Israel seven national memorial holidays, six of them were feasting events, and all six were eaten in joyful celebration to the Lord. Only the Day of Atonement was a day of fasting.[39] Israel's memorial celebrations are fulfilled in Jesus Christ as they all foreshadow him; his person or redemptive work on the cross of Calvary.

The altar was a place where the defilement of sin was off-scoured by sacrifice coupled with faith where the worshiper was made acceptable to God. The ashes of the animal sacrificed signaled divine acceptance as the

---

[37] John 1:36.
[38] See Luke 22:15-16.
[39] See Leviticus 16:29-31; 23:26-32 and compare the wording with Ps. 35:13-14; Isaiah 58:3-6, 13-14.

smoke ascended heavenward in a *"soothing aroma"* to God;[40] it is a picture of the separation of the spirit from the body[41] of flesh and meant the priest could continue into the tent of meeting on behalf of the worshiper into the presence of God. It is a picture of spiritual worship as Jesus spoke of with the Samaritan woman at the well;

"God is spirit, and those who worship Him must be led by the Spirit to worship Him

as He really is" (Jn. 4:23-24, Robert H. Mounce, "Jesus in His own Words").

Our participation in the celebration of the Lord's supper today recounts not only his death but more importantly his resurrected life by which we live, and share, and rejoice in the common-union of our life in him by the grace of God.

And that is reason to rejoice and *"celebrate the feast"* (I Cor. 5:7-8) with brothers and sister because this draws us together in Christ who has forgiven and recovered us unto our Father from the nations. Together we are the story of the Prodigal son[42] who has returned to his Father and He looks with great anticipation for our return so that He may throw a celebratory feast.

---

[40] Leviticus 1:9, 13, 17, et, al. All offerings are by fire on the altar, a soothing aroma, or sweet savor to the Lord.

[41] James 2:29, *"the body without the spirit is dead."*

[42] See, Luke 15:11-32.

When Paul and his fellow workers planted a church in a Gentile city,[43] they were dealing with strangers and aliens to the covenants of God with Israel, and consequently knew little to nothing of what that looked like or how to participate in them;

"...remember that at that time you were separate from Christ, excluded from citizenship in Israel and foreigners to the covenants of the promise, without hope and without God in the world" (Ephesians 2:12, NIV).

And the believers in Corinth were certainly no exception to that rule. But they soon learned what that meant, how it looked and how they were to behave once they were introduced into the household of God;[44]

"Consequently, you are no longer foreigners and strangers, but fellow citizens with God's people and also members of his household" (Eph. 2:19, NIV).

Paul also writes Timothy, a fellow worker he leaves in Ephesus, and say's;

"...but in case I am delayed, I write so that you will know how one should act (behave, or conduct himself) in the household of God, which is the church of the living God, the pillar and support of the truth" (I Tim. 2:15).[45]

---

[43] Romans 11:13; Galatians 1:16; 2:9.

[44] No doubt with the help of Jewish converts; see, Matt. 13:52, of the scribe in the kingdom of heaven.

[45] This is not replacement theology as some have claimed, it is fulfillment theology.

Parenthetically, Paul wrote both 1st and 2nd Corinthians from the city of Ephesus, where he spent over two years training men like Timothy and Titus and others to be workers, and church planters, Acts 19:8-10.[46]

This meant that these Gentile Christians had to learn, among other things, what a covenant meal looked like and how to properly participate in it. Paul spent some two years in Corinth (Acts 18:11) planting, teaching and raising up this church, and *"tearing down the dividing wall"* between Jew and Gentile (Eph. 2:14-18), in order that they may come together as one body in Christ and learn to partake of his life, and how to share His supper together as one new man; God's new society.

"The Lord's supper" (I Cor. 11:20), is unlike any other meal these new Gentile believers had ever eaten, and Paul contrasts this *supper* with:

First, the Jewish meals eaten during their divinely appointed festivals under the first covenant, especially the feast of Unleavened Bread and the Passover feast.[47]

Second, the meals they were accustomed to eating in the temples of idols.

---

[46] See "The Untold Story of the N.T. Church" by Frank Viola, 2004, 1st ed.; "The life and epistles of St. Paul" W.J. Conybeare, and J.S. Howson, 1968; "A harmony of the life of St. Paul" by Frank J. Goodwin, 1951; "Paul the Apostle" by Robert E. Picirilli, 1986.

[47] Other N.T. references of the Lord's Supper include, Acts 20:6; I Cor. 5:7-8; 10:16-18; 11:23-25.

Both of which Paul addressed directly in I Corinthians 10:14-33 in contrast to the Lord's supper addressed in 11:17-34.

Beginning in 10:14, the apostle writes, "Therefore, my beloved, flee from idolatry," as a warning not to get caught up in eating sacrificial meals to idols.

These new believers in the city of Corinth had lived in a culture steeped in satanic worship eating sacrificial meals offered to the idols of pagan deities in their temples. Continuing, the apostle believes them spiritually competent to judge between the cup and the bread as sharing in the body of Christ—the one cup and bread is synecdoche[48] for the meal shared among believers, just as Israel was one and all shared in the sacrifices of the altar in a covenant meal (10:16-18). Israel as "one body" partook of the "table of the Lord," v.21.

The significance of the one altar in which all Israel participated is fulfilled in the one cross in which all believers now participate. And just as the altar led to the table so too does the cross lead to the table of the Lord. At the table both Jew and Gentile come together as one body in Christ to celebrate, not his death, but his resurrection; his resurrected life in which they now share. Our Lord defeated the world forces of spiritual wickedness in heavenly places,[49] and all who come to him in faith are freed from the domain of Satan in the

---

[48] Synecdoche is a figure of speech using a part for the whole, i.e., cup and bread for an entire meal.
[49] Ephesians 6:12.

bondage of the slavery of sin[50] and are invited to eat at his covenant table.

It bears repeating, that this shared meal is a specific reference to the Passover feast, in which unleavened bread was eaten along with the roasted lamb, etc, as a family meal commemorating and celebrating Israels' deliverance from Egyptian bondage (Exodus 12).

Paul is saying, when you Gentiles lived apart from Christ and didn't know any better, those sacrifices made to idols were an offering to demons and eating that sacrificial meal in their temples or taking it home to eat was the same as eating a meal in honor of that idol-demon and being in covenant with them (vv.19-20, 27-29).

But now that you have been reconciled to Christ—**you know better**, and you certainly know you cannot possibly eat in those idols' temples at *"the table of demons"* and to do so is to *"provoke the Lord to jealousy"* (vv.21-22).[51]

To drink the Lord's cup and eat at his table indicates they were participating in a covenant meal with one another and with God just as the disciples did with the Lord Jesus at the last super, and in the next chapter the apostle explicitly refers to it as the Lord's supper;

---

[50] Colossians 1:13-14, 18, 20-22; 2:12-15.

[51] Hebrews 12:29, *"For our God is a consuming fire,"* and jealous for us, Zech. 8:2, as is Paul for his people, II Cor. 11:2.

"*Therefore, when you meet together, it is not to eat the Lord's supper...*" (v.20; but it certainly should have been, and that is Paul's point).

But then to turn around and drink "*the cup of demons*" and eat at "*the table of demons*" would be to participate in a covenant meal with those demons. This not only provokes the Lord to jealousy, but is highly offensive to the Jew, Gentile, and the ekklesia, v.32; the ekklesia is God's new man, a community of God's people who now bear the image of His Son.

Not only does it offend both Jewish and Greek brethren that have come into fellowship with one another around the table of the Lord, under his headship (11:3), you run the risk of offending your own conscience, and even the conscience of the unbeliever, 10:23-30.

The conclusion of chapter 10, vv.23-30, is very significant because it sets the stage for what follows in chapter 11.[52] No two chapters have been so badly misunderstood and taken out of context (proof texted) with regard to the Lord's supper than I Corinthians 10 and 11, which oddly enough constitutes most of what the New Testament has to say on this matter of eating the supper.

Before we dive further into these two chapters to unravel and explain the context, we want to begin by stating, we are not saying a person is sinning if they do

---

[52] Verse 1 of chapter 11 is actually the concluding verse of chapter 10.

not see the Lord's supper as we do. We are not saying you are in jeopardy of losing your salvation if you do not eat the supper as a full meal. We are not saying God will stop loving you if you do not begin eating the Lord's supper as a family meal together.

You may ask; **"Then what are you saying?!"**

> First; we are saying that this is what God's word reveals to us. And that alone has settled it for many.

> Second; we are saying that the social element of eating together as God designed it creates an environment that draws everyone into an intimate togetherness of sharing, a *fellowship of community* (common-union), in a way that the traditional style simply cannot do. If fact it hinders it.

> Third; we are seeking God's highest intention. Which is to *"learn Christ"* according to Matthew 11:29, and be conformed to his image,[53] which is best done in community.

Therefore, what we are saying, and positively affirm, is that if you've inherited a religious tradition, you would do well to examine it in the light of God's word and his way. Concerning this, the prophet Jeremiah has said; *"I Know, O Lord, that a man's way is not in himself, nor is it*

---

[53] See Colossians 1:27; Galatians 3:19; Romans 8:29; 12:2.

in a man who walks to direct his steps" (10:23).[54] Furthermore, this open, face-to-face, close-knit fellowship we share at his table causes us to seek Christ in one another so as to be conformed to his image; unto the *"fullness of Christ,"* as we grow up in him (Eph. 4:13, 15).

This growing up into the fullness of Christ is nothing other than to be conformed to his image in whom we are made, aided by **our togetherness** and **one anothering;** *"fitted and held together"* to encourage, or *"stimulate one another to love and good deeds"* (Eph. 4:16; Heb. 10:24-25, respectfully).[55] The two greatest assets the Lord has given us toward genuine transformation is first—himself, and then—one another.

The Lord's supper isn't a gimmick to draw people into our fellowship, nor should we use it as a wedge issue to divide brethren, unfortunately both of these have been used in these ways. Only when a body of believers seek together the Lord's mind on this matter will it be found. But many churches today are simply scared to look at this dimension of the Lord's supper much less put it into practice. And as we've said earlier; Christianity is meant to be experienced; it's a full contact sport. It's not a theology, it's a lifestyle. Christianity is the expression of God's nature in the world in a real and living way by those

---

[54] See also Isaiah 55:8-9.

[55] "58 to 0" (How Christ leads through the one-anothers), by Jon Zens, Graham Wood, editors; 2013.

who live by the indwelling life of Christ. The ekklesia is God's option to all that is in the world.

Part of living the Christian life is sharing the Lord with fellow believers at his supper, which is inherently participatory and experiential due to the indwelling life of Christ in each believer and it should never be reduced to a mere ceremony of outward "sacrament"

regulated exclusively to one man who alone has supposedly been endowed with the ability to transform the bread into the "flesh" of Jesus Christ and the wine into his "blood" as is practiced only in the Roman Church.

On the other hand, the supper should not be regulated to a five-minute silent ritual with a snippet of bread and sip of grape juice with everyone imagining Jesus' bloody body nailed to the cross suffering all over again for our sins. Like it or not, the main differences between these two scenarios played out between the Roman Church and Evangelical Churches really only amounts to changing the bread and wine through transubstantiation. Neither one of these practices matches the long-established biblical examples of what a covenant meal looks like and its divine intention.

Learning Jesus (as mentioned above) is what it means to *worship in spirit and truth."* [56] Jesus is the living word of truth, and when we come to know him in a real living experience with one another we enter into a deeper relationship with him (Jn. 14:6), and it is by him we come

---

[56] Matt. 11:29; Jn. 4:23-24; Eph. 4:20; 5:10.

to know the Father, as our own Father (Jn. 6:44-45; 20:17). We should patiently bear this in mind when discussing the differences of a full supper vs. the traditional "chip and sip" Lord's supper, because what we are after is not just working toward a better understanding but a deeper, more intimate spiritual relationship with the Lord Jesus and with one another, *Psalms 42:7.

It is at this very meal, around an open and interactive table (as we see Jesus doing not only at the "last supper" but every other meal he was involved in) where we can together experience joyful fellowship in the Lord, and this can't be done, it won't be done at the traditional symbolic table because everyone sits in silence in their pews, separated and contemplating their own sins while imaging Jesus once again on the cross of Golgotha. Such an approach adopts an attitude that is far more funeralistic in character than celebratory, much less participatory in nature.

Why then do we imagine our Lord dead on the cross every first day of the week while eating a "supper" dedicated to him? Brethren, we're doing this because we've inherited it from none other than the Roman Catholic tradition. (We'll expose those roots more fully in our next chapter).

After his resurrection Jesus appeared to his disciple still locked away and hiding in the upper room in order to reveal the truth of what the prophets had spoken about him; "While they still could not believe it because of their joy and amazement, He said to them, 'Have you *anything here to eat?'"* (Luke 24:41). Right, the first thing he does after calming their fears (that he was not a ghost), is start eating.

The Context of I Corinthians 11

At the time Paul writes the first Corinth[57] letter the church is about five years old. Paul planted the church as recorded in Acts 18, and is now ministering in the city of Ephesus. He learns of the various problems in Corinth through Chloe's people, I Cor. 1:11.

Corinth was a thoroughly Greco-Roman pagan culture, and Paul spent a full eighteen months there with a handful of other church workers planting and raising up this church.[58] With this in mind, it is difficult to comprehend how Paul and the other church workers like Silas, Timothy and Apollos could have taught and demonstrated the Lord's supper as eating a mere chip of unleavened bread and sipping a thimble full of wine in a silent, joyless memorial while imagining Jesus dying on the cross for their sins, only to have it blow up into a full meal where some got drunk and filled while others went away thirsty and hungry.

---

[57] The Corinth church was planted in approximately 52 AD and Paul writes to them in about 57 AD. There appears to have been a letter written to Paul from the church in Corinth but is now lost to us.

[58] Church workers in Corinth included Silas, Apollos, Timothy, Priscilla and Aquila, Stephanas and his household, Fortunatus, Achaicus, Barnabas, and others, including Peter and his wife may have spent time in Corinth; see Acts 18; I Cor. 1:12; 3:22 and chapter 16 for those named.

No one could have possibly gone away hungry and thirsty (much less full and drunk) if all the supper amounted to was a mere "sip and chip" as virtually all modern churches interpret this text and practice it as such.

Based upon the two most prominent interpretations and widely practiced "Lord's supper" today, we are faced with two very distinct options:

#1. The Roman Catholic dogma of "transubstantiation" as a "sacrament" of the Church performed exclusively by an ordained Roman priest during the consecration ritual of the "Mass" wherein a singular small circular "Host", a prefabed unleavened piece of bread[59] called the "eucharist"[60] is eaten, and is said to be the "real flesh" and "real blood" of Christ, although it remains under the appearance of bread and wine. And by eating this "transubstantiated" wafer-host the very body and blood of Christ is infused into the bodies and souls of those who eat it, thus receiving salvation. Additionally, to intentionally miss the Mass and the reception of the Host is to commit a mortal sin.

#2. The evangelical method of a memorial only "Lord's supper" is served from a symbolic communion table by two or more men who thank God for the sacrifice of

---

[59] The blessed or sanctified "Host" is served to the parishioner from a Chalice and the unused hosts are kept in a covered chalice called a "Ciborium" stored in a "Tabernacle" on or behind the altar table.

[60] "Eucharist" is the Greek word for "give thanks" or "thanksgiving" as used in I Cor. 11:24. It has become a loaded term full of theological meaning imagined by Roman Catholicism. It is classic eisegesis.

Jesus and pray God's blessing upon the unleavened bread and fruit of the vine, passed on small silver or wooden trays and cuplets to a muted and very somber audience who eat a mere chip of the bread and sip the cuplet of juice while remembering the guilt of their sins for which Jesus died and whose sins put him on the cross. The bread remains bread, the juice remains juice and are merely symbolic of the Lord's body and blood, eaten in "remembrance" of him.

It is worth pointing out, that many modern churches, especially mega churches, as a matter of convenience offer the "Lord's supper" of bread and grape juice in a sanitary perforated plastic container. Each person comes forward, takes one and returns to his seat to eat it alone with his thoughts, in silence. To enhance the experience the electric shades are drawn, the lighting dimmed and soft mood music is played in the background to keep the atmosphere quiet and somber.

Of course, there is a **3rd** option, and it is radically different than anything else being practiced in churches today. It is the one we have been advocating for throughout this book and is the only one that can actually be read about in the pages of the Bible.

Our homes are where we eat family meals and that is what the Lord's supper is, a family meal eaten together with other believers. Jesus inaugurated the new covenant community with this meal at the "last supper," which is the fulfillment of the Passover.

This 3rd option is described in Acts 2:41-47; 20:6-11; I Cor. 11:17-34, and the Gospel accounts of the "last supper." You simply cannot eat a family meal seated in a pew staring at the back of someone else's head and expect to have a meaningful relationship with them.

The problem in Corinth is not that they had turned the Lord's supper into a common meal, but that they had turned it into their "own meal." We read;

> "For everyone tries to grab his food before everyone else, with the result that one goes hungry and another has too much to drink!" (I Cor. 11:21; The New Testament in modern English, J. B. Phillips).

In every translation of that verse the problem is defined; they had turned the communal supper of the Lord into a private meal. They were not just eating a mere chip and sip that was over in a few short minutes, but had come together to eat a full meal just as those in Troas in Acts 20:7-11. We read;

> "On the first day of the week, when we gathered together to break bread, Paul began talking to them, intending to leave the next day, and prolonged his message until midnight. There were many lamps in the upper room where we were gathered together."

Notice it is the first day of the week that they gathered together. Verse 6 indicates it was their intention to gather together on that day, and for the purpose of "breaking bread,"[61] which as we have pointed out is the Lord's supper and means to "eat a meal."

This meal together lasted well into the evening hours, beyond the midnight hour so that lamps were lite, v.8. And after the young man Eutychus fell out of the 3rd floor window dead, Paul "resuscitated" him back to life, they went back up and again *broke the bread* (v.11). This meal lasted even beyond the midnight hour!

I Cor. 11:20 tells us explicitly that one of the main reasons for the Corinthians meeting together was to eat the Lord's supper, which is an inherently communal meal. Stated in the negative, v.20 reads;

> *"Therefore, when you meet together, it is not to eat the Lord's supper."*

It should have been, but given the way in which they were treating one another how could it be? Piggishly eating their *"own supper"* (v.21) and not waiting for everyone to arrive so that they could eat together.

Verse 21 is in sharp contrast to v.20; you have gathered together to eat the Lord's supper but some are full while others go hungry. The Lord's supper is not a private meal but an inherently communal meal.

The meaning is clear, don't start eating before everyone has arrived so that you can eat together and "share-and-

---

[61] The Gk. wording for "break bread" did not carry a religious meaning, it was common everyday language that meant to eat a meal, see Acts 27:34-38.

share alike" in the supper. Because they were not doing this, they had created division (v.18), internal factions in the body arose (v.19).

These factions are defined in verse 22, between the "Have's and the Have Not's." Specifically, those with food and home vs. those with no food or home. The Have's "despised"[62] the Have Not's who were not financially self-supportive and relied on the generosity of those in the church who could provide food and a home in which to meet.

We again point out this specific Greek word used in verses 20 and 21 is "deipnon" (supper), and means, "to take the principle meal of the day, an evening meal, a full meal or feast." This is what the church had gathered together to "eat"—it was not a private meal, but a communal meal, v.22 tells them where to eat a private meal, and v.34, "at home"! Those who were not waiting for their brethren to arrive before eating were admonished to eat at home. Eat what? Their own supper. When you meet together it is to eat the Lord's supper, and that is Paul's finial solution stated in vv.33-34;

> "So then, my brethren when you come together to eat, wait for one another. If anyone is hungry, let him eat at home, so that when you come together it will not be for judgment."

---

[62] The Have's held the Have Not's in *contempt*. The cultural context is that the economically superior looked down on the economically inferior. See "Making a meal of it" by Ben Witherington III, 2007.

Verses 23-25 has Paul recounting the last supper Jesus shared with his disciples, which was a Passover supper. Let's notice the order: [63]

>   **First**, v.23, the Lord *"took bread"*

>   **Second**, v.24, *"he broke it"*

>   **Third**, v.25, *"he took the cup after supper"*

Between the breaking of bread and the drinking of the cup a *supper* was eaten.

What Supper?! The Lord's supper, which is the fulfillment of the Passover supper.

Remember that word refers to a full meal. And that meal was what the Corinthians had met together to eat but were neglecting to wait for one another so as to eat together and share in it equally.

Two Suppers?

"In the same way He took the cup after supper saying..." (I Cor. 11:25a);[64] one of the explanations we have heard from brethren attempting to defend the traditional silent "chip and sip" supper is that there was "a supper within a supper." Or, that there was "a supper after the supper," as if there were somehow two suppers.

_____

[63] Compare Paul's account with Matthew's in 26:26-28.

[64] Paul's sequence of events of the "last supper" appears to follow Luke's Gospel (Lk. 22:19-20).

Paul plainly stated that they had turned the "*Lord's supper*" into their "*own supper*" (v.21) by not waiting for one another (v.33) to share in the communal meal. That alone knocks in the head the idea that there were "two suppers"—something Paul clearly opposed.

There is but one supper when the church comes together (vv.18, 20), so it surely cannot be "a meal within a meal" or, "a meal after the meal" as some have suggested. As if one meal is the symbolic Lord's supper (chip and sip style), and the other is a full course family meal.

Verse 25, "*after supper*" is the same supper, not a different one. Did Jesus have two suppers at the last supper with His disciples? Clearly, He did not.

It is one singular meal, not two different meals, and certainly not a "symbolic meal" followed by a "full meal" whether before, after, or during. It was one singular meal that included the unleavened bread and the fruit of the vine in the course of eating that last Passover supper together. That is the "*supper*" Paul is referring to in v.25.

The overall context of I Corinthians chapters 10 and 11, as well as the texts of Acts 2 and Acts 20 previously covered, and the Gospel accounts consistently show that the Lord's supper is the fulfillment of the Passover, which was a covenant meal shared by God's believing community who were delivered from the bondage of Egyptian captivity. Today (from the first century onward), it is called the Lord's supper and we are the continuation of God's believing community who have been delivered from the bondage of a demonic kingdom. We are God's Israel according to Galatians 6:16, and we too have a covenant meal.

Verse 26 informs us that "*as often as we eat this bread and drink the cup*"—the bread and cup are used as synecdoche; using parts for the whole, the singular for the plural. Just as I Cor. 10:16 uses the singular word "*cup*" for all cups that are used to drink the fruit of the vine from by every member of the body. The cup is a literal, physical drinking vessel but it is the content of the cup that is significant not the cup itself. The same is true of the bread also, it encompasses the whole, all bread that is broken in the supper of the Lord in all places, not just in Corinth.

This follows what Jesus said at the last Passover in Luke 22:17-19 concerning the drink and the bread. We all partake of the one bread; we all partake on the one cup. Just like I Cor. 12:16, if one member suffers, all suffer with the one. If one is honored all rejoice with the one. That's what the family community does, it acts as one for the good of all to the glory of Christ (see also, Romans 12:15).

The one bread is the Lord's body for all, the drink is the Lord's blood for all. Just as the church is one in Christ (Eph. 4:4-6), and all participate in sharing the word and the food at his one table around which all gather to eat and rejoice in their resurrected life in Christ.

When we eat this bread and drink this cup together, we "*proclaim the Lord's death until he comes*" again (v.26). In this there is a past, present, and future aspect to sharing the supper together. Recall the words of Exodus 12:14 that predicts a fulfillment of this day of deliverance;

> "Now this day will be a memorial to you; and you shall celebrate it as a feast to the Lord; throughout your generations you are to celebrate it as a permanent ordinance."

So, although it's a *memorial* it is also a *celebration* and a *feast* and that's not sad! And it carries on *throughout your generations*, that is, it continued on with God's new covenant people. A *celebration* that lasts as a *permanent ordinance* until the Lord's return.

And notice Ex. 12:27, that it was originally eaten in their homes (and thereafter too). Let that sink in. Then reread Acts 2:42...the Passover meal was not eaten at the temple or the Synagogue, or a church building, it was eaten at home with the family.

The context of I Cor. 11:27 shows us that to eat the supper in an "unworthy manner" is directly related to their not waiting for one another to arrive in order to eat together, instead some (the "unapproved", v.19b) selfishly ate their "own supper first" (v.21) without sharing. That is what it means to eat (the bread) and drink (the cup) in an unworthy manner. The passage is not addressing one's inner character or how their living, the apostle has already addressed that issue in chapter 5 concerning the man who "has his father's wife" [65] and

---

[65] Most agree this to be his step-mother, his father's second wife.

their overall attitude toward him and his sin; it was leaven.

Concerning *"that man"*, he is to be disfellowshipped from the ekklesia and delivered back into the world which is Satan's domain; *"for the destruction of his flesh that his spirit may be saved in the day of the Lord Jesus"* (I Cor. 5:5-6). Cleaning out the sinful leaven preserves the lump of dough in holiness to God. Expelling this man from the body and adjusting your attitudes toward such sinful behavior allows you to *"celebrate the feast"* in *"sincerity and truth"* (v.8). *"For Christ our Passover Lamb has been sacrificed"* (v.7).

To eat the Lord's supper in an *"unworthy manner"* (11:27) was the result of not waiting for one another to arrive so as to eat together and share in the supper. It is the opposite of eating in *"sincerity and truth"* (5:8b). The correspondence between these two texts is unmistakable; **1)** Known, open rebellious sin cannot remain in the body. **2)** Eating in an *unworthy*[66] manner is not waiting for one another to arrive, turning the Lord's supper into your *"own supper"* (v.21).

Both the Lord's supper and the church meeting together in face-to-face fellowship is inherently communal, it is not a matter of cliques. The communal nature of the ekklesia is to reflect the very nature of the trinitarian

---

[66] *Unworthily* is an adverb meaning criminally "liable," "chargeable", or "guilty." It is a judicial term meaning you are answerable to God for the abuse; "you bear responsibility."

community of God; Father, Son and Holy Spirit. And we are to express His life together.

The guilt incurred (v.27) is a result of not waiting for one another in eating and drinking together and treating the Lord's supper as your own supper. The Lord's supper is unlike any other meal, it is a covenant meal of peace and reconciliation with our Father in Christ and with one another regardless of race or gender.

To the casual observer this meal may look like any other, but the significance of the bread and wine in this meal represents our Lord's body and blood and should not be treated as common. Judas treated the "last supper" with contempt and he incurred the judgment of God as a result. Judas had not set his mind on the things of the Lord but gave himself over to his lust for riches so that Satan entered him. Without properly understanding the importance of the Passover, as fulfilled in Christ (I Cor. 5:7), and everyone's part in sharing it as one body in Christ, we lose its significance.

Verse 28 tells us to *"examine ourselves"*—and there are 3-simple-points to this:

1. V.21-22; Relatedness. Relatedness to our sisters and brothers with whom we're gathered without regard to social or economic status.
2. V.28 and 33; Examination. Examine yourself in relation to the brethren, that all are present and sharing the Lord and His supper in togetherness.

3. V.29 and 31; Discernment. To *"judge the body rightly"*[67] is to discern the body of believers you are gathered together with. It is not the body of Jesus Christ that is under consideration, it is the body of believers, the church, the ekklesia.

This matter of eating the supper in a worthy manner *"from house to house"* (Acts 2:46) was how, and why the church gatherings were kept intentionally small in numbers. The potential for abuse in large gatherings as experienced in Corinth[68] is far more likely to occur in larger church gatherings where it is inherently more difficult to exercise your gifts, and proper leadership and teach the ethics of kingdom behavior,[69] especially among newly converted worldly pagans.

There is debate as to whether or not v.30 refers to physical death or spiritual death when it says *"a number sleep"* due to the abuse of the supper going on in Corinth. There are good arguments on both sides on the meaning of this verse.

To take it at face value means "physical death" and this is the way Paul used it in his writings elsewhere; I Cor. 15:6, 51; I Thess. 4:13-15.

---

[67] V.29, Paul says to discern "the body," he does not mention the blood, or the Lord himself.

[68] Table abuse also occurred in the large gathering at Antioch Syria as recorded in Galatians 2:11-14.

[69] Church History reveals this is why the supper was reduced to a "chip & sip" sacrament, so that control could be exercised by a ruling clergy class that developed through the third and fourth centuries.

But it did not come without warning. It was preceded first by becoming physically weak, followed by becoming physically sick. If these antecedent conditions weren't enough to awaken you to the spiritual danger you were in, death followed.

They were to discern the body gathered around the table. By waiting for one another they would not eat in an *"unworthy manner"*—which was a flagrant disregard for the body of Christ, not a piece of bread on the table, but the body of believers at the table, as spoken of in 10:17; *"...there is one bread, we who are many are one body and we all partake of the one bread."* And also, 12:27; *"Now you are Christ's body, and individual members of it."*

If the modern evangelical churches interpretation and practice of eating the Lord's supper from I Corinthians 10 and 11 is correct, that it is merely a "symbolic meal" consisting of only a chip of unleavened bread and a sip of the fruit of the vine, how could anyone **not** go away hungry?! Moreover, why would anyone have to wait for another if only a crumb of bread and a sip of wine are sufficient?

The supper as practiced today is eaten individually, and as isolated from one another as you can get without leaving the auditorium, because it is between the individual and the Lord, right? In which case would we not be better off eating it in a corner, or tucked away in a closet to ensure there are absolutely no distractions so you can be completely focused on your sins, and your personal "worthiness" before the Lord?

However, if the Lord's supper is intended to be an actual meal where all could eat freely in an open face-to-face fellowship at a real table (not a symbolic table), and be satisfied, then no one could go away hungry, or thirsty, glutted or drunk! Because you have done as v.31 says; *"If we* (plural) *judged ourselves* (plural) *rightly, we* (plural) *would not be judged."* Having judged *ourselves* rightly we eat "worthy" before the Lord and cannot be condemned along with the world, v.32.

Vv.31-32 taken together; it is a dynamic interactive congregational action that is taking place where all are made worthy in their behavior toward one another.

V.33, *"So then my brethren, when you come together to eat…"*, that is, when the body comes together, they are to discern the spiritual health of the body, and so insure everyone is present in order to participate. How? *"…wait for one another."*

Contrary to popular opinion and practice as we have said, "church" is not a spectator sport it is a full contact participatory sport. This *"discerning, or judging"* is an all for one, and one for all activity of *"the whole body"* (as Eph. 4:14-16, describes body life).

Paul has already addressed the matter of sin in the body, being likened to leaven in the bread dough (I Cor. 5). They were advised to remove him before he spoils the entire loaf of bread, i.e., the body of Christ. That activity involves the entire church (not just the elders, or pastor, Board of Directors, etc), the entire body is active in the discipline of the immoral man. They were not to have table fellowship with such a person involved in active, open sinful behavior. We are to judge (discern) those within the church, not outside the church (5:12-13). So that we are not condemned along with the world (11:32).

If every church in America today (regardless of the denomination) would begin to gather together in their homes after their corporate "worship service" to eat the Lord's supper as a family meal around their dining room table I believe we would witness a more involved church, a stronger and more unified and spiritually vibrant church that would certainly have a greater impact on the culture and society at large, simple because this carries a built in evangelization quality among the "laity" that can't be denied or ignored.

As we bring the section of our study to a conclusion we would like to add, correcting our practice of the Lord's supper alone is not the "silver bullet" to building a healthy, robust, interconnected ekklesia, it involves the disciple aspect as well (individually and corporately). In that we must recognize the ekklesia of God is a spiritual body of believers, just as the supper of the Lord is a spiritual meal. It is not a gathering of car enthusiasts, or fishing buddies, or the local book club—it is a gathering of disciples and believers committed to knowing by experience the Lord Jesus Christ, and sharing Him in the supper with one another as described in I Cor. 11. While at the same time, what's also described in chapters 12, 14 and 16 is taking place; it is not a stand-alone issue. That is, it is not "separate and apart" (c-o-cer's will know what I mean by that phrase).

So far, we have addressed in some detail the two most commonly practiced types of the Lord's supper. These two forms are similar in that they meet together in an auditorium style pew seating all facing forward without any interaction during the tray passing, or a going forward to receive the eucharist.

We've shown that the "sacramental style" of Lord's supper which involves "transubstantiation" is absolutely contrary to Scripture. In fact, there is no need for such a thing, seeing that the life of the resurrected Lord Jesus Christ already indwells each genuine believer by faith;[70] all of him in all of us and growing up in Him (Eph. 4:13). So, eating something of his "real flesh" and drinking his "real blood" in some small portion is counter-intuitive and a contradiction to the entire narrative of Scripture concerning the all sufficiency of Christ. It is also a contradiction of the "once for all" passages of Hebrews 9:26; 10:10, 12, and 14.

For those of the Roman Catholic persuasion who insist on the "sacrament" of the "eucharist" and the dogma of "transubstantiation" (performed by only an ordained Roman priest), it is difficult to find any middle ground of agreement on which to be united in Christ. Such insistence actually hinders the unity of the church as one body (Eph. 4:4).

At the same time, we would also like to point out that among Protestant churches, neither should the supper

---

[70] John 6:47; 11:25; 14:6; I John 5:11-12, more will be explained concerning the "bread of life" at the conclusion of the book.

be a mere 10-minute silent ritual as practiced among evangelical churches today. The evangelical's insistence on their model of the Lord's supper is equally misplaced, although it does not change the substance of the bread and wine as does Catholicism, it has nevertheless adopted its form and truncated practice of the supper from the medieval Roman Church practice.

"Send out thy light and thy truth; let them lead me...", Psalms 43:3. Jesus is truth embodied and He brings light to our darkened minds to illuminate Him as the Way (KJV).

"Deep calls unto Deep...", Psalms 42:7. God is calling us to an ever-deeper relationship that can never be exhausted, in this life or the next. It is a relationship of experience.

Chapter 3

A Practical Practice of the Lord's Supper

(An Un-ritualistic way of sharing his meal)

"In most churches today, many people are ready

for change, provided nothing is different."

--author unknown

Any book on the Bible should be part exegesis and part story telling. Here's a part of the story.

When we're invited over to eat at a close friend's house, to a brother or a sister's home, we don't normally get dressed up, it's more of a "a come as you are" situation. In fact, it's about as far from formal as you can get, it's very casual, comfortable and relaxed. On a warm summer day, we may even wear a T-shirt and shorts, capris, or a sun dress with sandals or flip-flops.

This is every Lord's supper and gathering of the church. No dress-up, no production, no special building or ceremonial rituals performed. In fact, no two Lord's suppers are ever the same. Just as no two dinners, luncheons or suppers were the same with Jesus, and there were a number of dining events Jesus attended during his earthly ministry, and they were all quite informal and very casual.

So often was Jesus seen out eating and drinking he was accused of being a *"drunkard and a glutton."*[71] You might say it was his favorite pastime. But even the Baptist was somewhat bothered by this, and while imprisoned he sent some disciples to ask him, *"Are you the expected one, or shall we look for someone else?"* (Matt 11:2-3). Jesus was not exactly what John (and many others) expected from the Messiah of God. But Jesus' answer certainly satisfied him,[72] cryptic though it may appear to us.

When it comes to the "last supper" it covers five whole chapters 13-through-17 in the Gospel of John. In chapter 13, verses 12, 23, 25 and 28 are the "reclining" verses.[73] Now that's some casual dining!

When we've been invited to someone's home to eat, upon arrival we're warmly greeted and invited in. Our host has chosen the dishware and provided the food and drink, although they may ask their guests to bring a side-dish. Couples will sit together and the rest will sort of fill in where it's comfortable for them. Typically, the host will lead everyone in a prayer of thanksgiving as the meal begins. There may even be a toast made in the course of

---

[71] See Matt 11:19; Luke 7:34; Deuteronomy 21:20 on gluttony and drunkenness.
[72] See Matt 11:4-19; Lk. 7:21; Isaiah 35:4-5. Suggested reading, "Prisoner in the third Cell", G. Edwards.
[73] We could also include verse 4, as it implies Jesus first got up from reclining at the table. Throughout the Gospels there are many *"reclining"* verses. It implies liberty as opposed to standing in service.

the meal. Different conversations will go on throughout the meal, most at the same time, although the host may center everyone's attention on a particular topic or two. In rare occurrences if anyone is rude, or gets out of hand, they'll be politely invited to leave.

This is a brief, but close description of how the "last supper" went. Jesus is host of this supper (a Passover meal) that he would share with his twelve closest friends. He had preplanned where this meal would be eaten, nothing fancy, just whatever the owner of that upper guest room had for dishware, furnished with low couches on which to comfortably recline while eating, and a customary foot washing basin. A couple of the Lord's disciples (Peter and John) were asked by Jesus to go into Jerusalem and make final preparations of lamb and the rest of the meal for everyone attending (see, Luke 22:7-13).

Now let's notice some things missing in the Gospel narratives of the last supper.

~Jesus gives no long draw-out liturgy to be repeated thereafter.

~There is no indication of a special "chalice" from which they all drank.

~There are no special ornate garments worn, by anyone.

~There is no sanctuary, just an ordinary upper guest room.

~There are no pews, a podium, or special chairs.

~There are no silver trays with wafers of unleavened bread.

~There is no altar (table), just a simple ordinary dining table.

~There is an ordinary loaf of unleavened bread that is shared, no wafer-hosts.

~They are not eating in silence.

~And most of all, Jesus doesn't perform transubstantiation with the unleavened bread, or any semblance of a Mass.[74]

Obviously, none of these things were a part of that supper or any that followed, in fact, there is no mention of any of that stuff anywhere in all the New Testament writings, or of a Mass or transubstantiation. Nor a silent ritual. All such things have been developed over eons of time and incorporated into the modern church system.

Did Jesus really expect his disciples to repeat a highly formal ritualistic ceremony at every Lord's supper until his return? Moreover, one that bears no resemblance to

---

[74] "Mass" comes from the Latin "Misa"—meaning to send, or dismiss at the end of the performance. This term came to be used after the 5th century. See, Catechism of the Catholic Church, 2nd ed. 1997; The Catholic Church, a concise history, by Barrie R. Strauss, 1992.

the one he shared with his disciples. It's the original "Groundhog's Day"![75]

In reality what we find is actually just the opposite of anything resembling a liturgical Mass, or a silent ritual of tray passing. There is no real or imagined crucifix hanging over a symbolic communion table or an altar table, none of that is found in any of the Gospel narratives or anywhere else in the N.T. So why do it? If God wanted it, and it were that important to Him He could have easily shown it to us by having Jesus perform it. Or at least one of the apostles thereafter perform it.

Can we go back to an Acts 2 description of a house-to-house fellowship where Christ is central to our lives especially when we gather together to eat his supper and remember his awesome sacrifice that reunites us back to the Father?

The Lord's supper properly understood is a covenant meal just as was the Israelite Passover was a covenant meal. One that recalled their emancipation from Egyptian bondage as the supper today recalls our emancipation from Satanic bondage. While at the same time it is a covenant meal that celebrates our reunion back to God as our Father in Christ Jesus; He the Lamb of God.

It is not a religious ceremony, it is a celebratory spiritual meal together that recalls not only his sacrifice on the cross of Calvary, but his entire life of self-sacrifice and

_____

[75] Pop-culture movie reference to Bill Murry's "Groundhog's Day."

his resurrected, ascended, and indwelling life in his people, the ekklesia.

We are short-changing ourselves by turning the Lord's supper into a silent 10-minute, mournful ritual that imagines him back on the cross. This procedure also cheats the Lord who is host of the meal from interacting with his people in a real and meaningful way.

To worship in *"spirit and truth"* as Jesus said to the Samaritan woman at the well, is to worship God in a real and living way, in honesty, and in open face-to-face fellowship. And worship is 24/7 for the Christian according to Romans 12:1-2; *"...present your bodies a living and holy sacrifice to God, which is your spiritual service of worship."*

Robert H. Mounce's, "Jesus in His Own Words", renders John 4:23-24;

"A time is coming; in fact, it's already here, when true worshippers will be led by the Spirit to worship the Father as he really is. And the Father wants to be worshiped like that. God is spirit, and those who worship him must be led by the Spirit to worship him as he really is." [76]

We should ask ourselves;

---

[76] Robert H. Mounce, "Jesus in His Own Words" B&H Pub. Gp. Nashville TN., 2010, cpwrt. 2010.

~Did Jesus ever participate in any kind of a purely symbolic meal?

~Is there a type or shadow in the Old Testament where Israel ever ate a purely symbolic meal ("a chip and sip") that we could point to as a specific fulfillment of the Lord's supper as practiced in evangelic churches today?

~Did any of the Apostles teach or participate in a purely symbolic meal?

~If not, why then do we practice the Lord's supper as a "purely symbolic" meal?

On teaching the Lord's supper many Christians miss the point of "experience." Christianity isn't a theology so much that it is an experiential learning process. It is a practice of living what you've learned.

Many Christians are stuck in the theology department and rarely move into the experience department, because they have grown accustomed to the pew and never move to the table so as to actually experience a real, interactive, experiential table of the Lord with their brethren. The majority of Christians today chop up their Christianity into little segments of time, giving an hour (sometimes two) to the Lord on Sunday morning, a bit more on Wednesday evening and a moment of two before each meal. The rest of their time is completely taken up by and absorbed in whatever life pursuit they fancy.

The table of the Lord is an experience that most Christians will never have, just as many will never experience a baptism of full submersion and all that goes with these.

Nevertheless, this is all that is taught and exampled in the pages of the Bible—which is why we've subtitled this book; "It's not what you think." It's not what you think because it's not what you do, because "we practice what we believe and believe what we practice." (And we don't practice that because we don't believe it!) We cannot practice differently until we know differently; only when we know different will we do different.

The Lord's supper is modeled for us in only one way throughout Scripture, as an "all hands-on deck" full, participatory, interactive meal. And unless you've personally experienced that you don't know what you're missing. It is to know by experience, not in theory.

You can't "gainsay it" or contradict it—how can you, you've never experienced it. Scripture certainly doesn't contradict it; we've demonstrated that rather conclusively.

All you are left with is a flat denial, but only because you've never done it and your church (the one you probably grew up in) doesn't practice it that way. (Yeah, we know).

All we are saying is what the Bible says, which is God's revelation of Himself to us so that we know His eternal purpose and may participate in it. Which, in short, is to conform us to the image of His only begotten Son, the Lord Jesus Christ. And one of the many ways He accomplishes that is through table fellowship where we share and share alike in the multifaceted blessings God bestows upon us around His table toward that end.

Jesus Christ is the conclusion to Israel's history as God's son[77] and all of that covenant according to Rom. 10:4 and II Cor. 3:6, 16, et., al. "He completes and resolves Israel's history," as Scott McKnight put it. This is especially seen in the Lord's supper because as the Passover lamb he unites all of us in the Father as His new covenant people around His table;

> "On this mountain the Lord of hosts will make for all peoples a feast of rich food, a feast of well-aged wine, of rich food full of marrow, of aged wine well refined. And he will swallow up on this mountain the covering that is cast over all nations. He will swallow up death forever; and the Lord will wipe away tears[78] from all faces, and the reproach of his people he will take away from all the earth, for the Lord has spoken. It will be said on that day, 'Behold, this is our God; we have waited for him, that he might save us. This is the Lord; we have waited for him; let us be glad and rejoice in his salvation'" (Isaiah 25:6-9, ESV).

The table is basic to our habitat;

---

[77] See, Exodus 4:22.
[78] See, Revelation 21:3-4.

"On either side of the river was the tree of life, bearing twelve crops of fruit, yielding it's fruit every month … come, let the one who is thirsty take of the water of life without cost" (Revelation 22:2a, 17b).

Chapter 4

The Rise of Transubstantiation in the Lord's Supper

(A general discussion on transubstantiation of the Lord's Supper from history)

"A lie gets half way around the world

before truth gets it's boots on."

--author unknown

Two distinguishing marks of the church in the first century was the believer's baptism and sharing the Lord's supper. These expressions of faith are well attested to throughout both testaments of the Bible as we have shown above.

As Augustine rightly put it;

> *"In the old the new concealed; in the new the old revealed."* [79]

Midway into the second century the church began to move along two distinct parallel lines; one branch became unmistakably institutional and organizational, while the other remained largely organic and natural. By the mid-

---

[79] Augustine of Hippo, AD 345-430.

4th century however, the distinction between the institutional and organic church became quite sharp. Along with that the distinction between church and state was completely eradicated, as a result "religious law" was enforced by "civil law."

This was due in part because the institutional Church took up residence in "the eternal city of Rome," and began to adopt the Roman empirical governmental structure. As a result, it reverted back to its Roman roots of a hierarchical order of ecclesiastic clergymen that was practiced in pagan temples and began to assume titles and power associated with their position. All of which mirrored the Roman empire hierarchical order. Eventually the institutional Church assumed the name, "The Holy Roman Catholic Church"[80]—because it was wholly Romanized!

Distinctions

The **first** became more organizational, creedal, formal and ceremonial, special wardrobe, special buildings of worship.

The **other** largely remained organic, free of creeds and informal, humble, modest dress, and met in their homes.

The **first** began to develop a clergy class, religious specialists, a hierarchal priesthood.

---

[80] The Catholic Church still holds this same title today, though few remember it's Roman origins.

The **other** remained a brotherhood, a priesthood of all believers, brothers and sisters.

The **first** became culturally acceptable, acquired property, political power and used it to enforce ecclesiastical power, imposing even death on dissenters.

The **other** remained simply cultural influencers without any political power, disciplining only their own local member by disfellowship, never by death.

The **first** became universal in scope, everyone within a countries bounders were wards of the Church, forced attendance, and partaking of the "sacraments" was strictly enforced.

The **other** remained strictly local in scope, no forced attendance, no "sacraments," informal meetings, *river* baptisms and a simple informal meal called the Lord's supper.

The **first** drifted toward an empirical rule of one man as head of the church.

The **other** remained orientated on Jesus Christ as head of his church.

The institutional branch nearly persecuted and martyred the other out of existence, except for the fact that Jesus had promised that "*the gates of Hades will not overpower it*"—but the bloody horrors that the institutional Church inflicted on believing Christians has been extensively cataloged in such books as; "Foxe's Book of Martyrs" by John Foxe; "Martyrs Mirror" by Thieleman J. van Braght; "The Reformers and their Stepchildren" by Leonard Verduin; "The Secret of the Strength" by Peter Hoover; "To Glory in a Blaze" by J. R. Broome; "The Life of Jeanne Guyon" by T. C. Upham, and a host of other books written on this subject and about particular men and women who were persecuted and martyred through the centuries by the religious authorities of the institutional branch.

Once Christianity was legalized[81] and gained social acceptability it began to accumulate class influence and political power. This began in earnest in AD 312[82] under the new emperor Constantine, growing in both ecclesiastical and civil power exponentially through the succeeding centuries before it's civil powers mercifully died out in the 1700's. During that time however, the Roman Church unleashed some of the most gruesome and torturous deaths ever devised by man to be inflicted on his fellow man.[83]

And why were these monstrous death penalties carried out by the Institutional Church?

---

[81] The emperor of Rome, Galerius, first semi-legalized Christianity in AD 311 with the "edict of toleration."

[82] The new emperor of Rome, Constantine AD 312, actually favored Christianity over the other pagan religions and extended special privileges to it and the Romanization of the church began. See "Church History in Plain Language" by Bruce Shelly, 2nd edition, 1995.

[83] The inhuman deaths inflicted by the Roman Church also include The Inquisitions and The Crusades.

Because the Roman Church took to itself complete ecclesiastical authority that also acquired the authority of the civil magistrate to carry out civil penalties for any infraction they deemed worthy of punishment.[84]

During the Reformation years[85] there were two main reasons for this blood shed:

1. Men rediscovered personal faith and baptism by immersion for the adult for the remission of sins who could confess his or her faith in Christ, not infants by sprinkling.

2. Men began to repudiated the Roman Catholic Church and its authoritarian rule over their individual religious lives, and all of its institutional sacraments.[86] Including the Lord's supper and the notion of transubstantiation.

What spawned the Reformation and its counterpart the Radical Reformation?[87] The basic invention of the

---

[84] This entire 1,000-year era was known as the "Dark Ages." See "The Story of Civilization" by Will Durant, vol. 4 thru. 6, 1950.

[85] This era of Reformation (mid-1300's to the mid-1700's) came to be called the "Renaissance" and bridged the gap between the Dark Ages and Age of Enlightenment, aka the Renaissance; see https://www.history.com/topics/renaissance/renaissance.

[86] The 7 sacraments of the Roman Church; Baptism; Confirmation; Communion; Penance; Extreme Unction; Holy Orders; Marriage, from The Faith Explained Leo J. Trese, 4th print edition, 1969.

[87] The Anabaptists comprised the second front of reformationists; referred to as the Reformers Stepchildren. See "The Reformers and their Stepchildren" by Leonard Verduin.

Gutenberg printing press.[88] This made the Bible widely available to English speaking Europeans in their native language in mass for the first time in world history.[89] But this was not without great cost to those who translated the Bible from Hebrew, Greek and Latin into the English and German tongues, which was strictly forbidden by the Roman Church under penalty of death. Which the Church carried-out over some five hundred years against those whose only motivation was to speak and teach the Gospel of Jesus Christ as they understood the faith and their life in Christ.

Another factor that leads to the Reformation awakening was basic literacy. During the Dark Ages illiteracy was estimated at 90 to 95% of the entire European continent. This allowed the Roman Catholic Church to perpetrate its crimes of ecclesiastical malfeasance against the poor illiterate and unsuspecting population of Europe.

But with the rise of the Roman Catholic Church and its various multifaceted and peculiar doctrines came the doctrine of transubstantiation (which first gained prominence in 787 AD, but only became the official dogma of the Roman Church in 1215 AD,[90] and made retroactive back to the last supper), wherein the

---

[88] The Johann Gutenberg printing press, developed in the early 1400's.

[89] William Tyndale accomplished this great task at the cost of his own life on Friday, Oct. 6 1536. See "To Glory in a Blaze" cited above.

[90] "The Age of Faith" Will Durant, vol. 4, pgs. 741, 763, pub. 1950.

Catholic priest during the performance of the Mass changes the substantiative nature of the host, or wafer of unleavened bread (i.e., the "eucharist"), into the literal flesh of Jesus Christ with the blood in it, which is why the parishioner receives only the little host, because it is the literal flesh and blood of Christ, so the Roman Church contends.[91] And by eating the little wafer of bread they are supposedly being ushered again into salvation, this is why the Catholic Church teaches it is a "mortal sin" to intentionally miss the Sunday Catholic Mass, because you can't receive the eucharist, and with it salvation.[92]

This institutionalizing really amounts to a form of emotional and behavioral control with a heaping dose of guilt accompanied by fear that God will strike you down for intentionally missing the "Mass." This amounts to "sacramental salvation."

The transubstantiation (comes from two Latin words; "trans"—meaning across; and "substantiation"—meaning substance), occurs when the Catholic priest lifts the "eucharist" up during the performance of the Mass and the altar boy rings the little bells in order to get everyone's attention, to witness the "transubstantiation" taking place. At that moment, parishioners are required to look adoringly at the eucharist. The priest then announces in Latin; "hoc est

---

[91] Catechism of the Catholic Church, 2nd ed. 1997; Pt. 2, Article 3 section.

[92] The word "eucharist" is Latin for "thanksgiving," i.e., I Cor. 11:24, and tied directly to salvation.

corpus" meaning "this is the (my) body." Which to the English-speaking ear sounded like "hocus pocus."[93]

But then it is taught that even though it has been changed into the literal body and blood of Christ it is only in the "appearance of bread and wine." That is, "the color, taste, weight and shape of bread and wine, or whatever else appears to the senses, remains the same after the change of the entire substance of bread and wine into the body and blood of Christ."[94] And that is why my dear reader, it is called a "sacrament."[95] And according to the Roman Church, "the Sacraments" administered by the Catholic priest are what dispense salvation to the worshiper. It is not by faith in Jesus Christ through grace but through the Sacraments administered by the Roman priest.

So even though it still looks like, tastes like, and to every other sense appears like bread and wine, it is not, because the Ordained Roman priest has changed it in the performance of the "Mass" at the altar-table through the ritual of "transubstantiation" with the "sacramental" words "hoc est corpus"! This is reinforced as the priest say's to each parishioner, "the body of Christ"—that comes forward to receive the wafer. This phrase serves as a prompt for the parishioner to open his or her mouth,

---

[93] English Archbishop of Canterbury, John Tillotson popularized this clever twist in an Anti-Catholic tract in 1684.

[94] "Father Smith Instructs Jackson" by Archbishop J. F. Noll; revised by Rev. A. J. Nevins, Up. ed., 1975.

[95] According to the Roman Church a sacrament is an efficacious sign of grace by which divine life is dispensed by the Holy Spirit. Hence, by eating the host you receive divine life, see CCC, 2nd ed. 1997.

so that the priest may place it on their tongue. (Although now you may hold your hands out flat, one atop the other and take it yourself).[96]

It Begins with Grace through Faith in Christ Alone

This is where we would like to ask two questions:

—Where does a relationship with God begin?

—And how is it sustained?

There are numerous examples provided for us in the Gospels of where and how a saving relationship with God begins and continues, and not a one of them involves an intercessory Catholic Priest, a ceremonial Mass, a ritual Sacrament, or a transformed Eucharist. In a word, there is no institution or religious organization between you and Jesus Christ that meets out salvation.

The following are a few examples of *where and how* a relationship with God begins;

Mark 5:24-34, a woman with an issue of blood, a twelve-year hemorrhage. She's heard of Jesus (see, Lk. 6:17-19; 8:43-48) so she reasons to herself, *"If I can only get close enough to touch the hem of his cloak I'll be made well."*

---

[96] At one time, it was a "mortal sin" to intentionally touch the host. But that was changed in about 1980.

She's desperate and on the verge of being destitute, which meant death would not be far behind. She's run out of options. So, she squeezes through the crowd being jostled back and forth as she inches ever closer, defiling everyone she touches along the way due to the impurity of her flowing blood.

Leviticus 12 speaks of the impurity of a woman's issue of blood at childbirth, and 15:19-33 speaks of the woman's issue of blood and impurity associated with her menstrual cycle. Apparently, this woman's cycle was chronic. And during this period of blood flow, whatever the reason, whoever comes into contact with her is rendered unclean.

At last, she has maneuvered her way to within touching range of Jesus, and she just catches the hem of his garment with the tips of her fingers, and instantly her blood flow is stopped, she literally felt her body healed!

What shot through her mind; "Wow…I'm healed! For the first time…in twelve long years…I am well!" She was beside herself in delirious joy!

But the Lord felt it too and draws attention to the fact that power had gone out from him because someone had touched him.

In an instant a flush of panic struck her like a thunder clap.

In such a crowd, who wasn't touching him!? But he knows who it is, and she is petrified with fear knowing what she has done, defiling him and everyone else in that throng of people. Jesus quickly scans behind him for the culprit and singles her out, she throws herself at his feet in a tearful plea of mercy and confesses everything to him. But she receives far more than just mercy. She receives grace upon grace and overwhelming love from so gracious a Lord as Jesus, the great physician.

He smiles, and gently takes her hand to lift her up, and says, *"Daughter, your faith has made you well; go in peace and be healed of your affliction."*

Here is the center of her faith in living color, in the person of Jesus of Nazareth and her fellowship with him in than instant, in that intimate moment would lift her into the heavens one day. But for now, the heavens have been brought to her, to live in her, and she would live by that life.

This is where and how her relationship with God began. And there is no religious organization or ritual performance she is ever asked to take part in, or place her faith in —her faith would forever be placed in Christ Jesus. And nothing and no one would ever come between she and her Lord. Nor should it for you and I either.

It Continues by Grace through Faith in Christ Alone

Matthew 8:5-13; Luke 7:1-10,[97] gives us the account of a Centurion of the Roman army who came to Jesus in

---

[97] Some consider John 4:46-54 to be this account also.

Capernaum to implore him to come and heal his servant. The Lord's answer is emphatic; *"Of course, at once."* But the Centurion quickly added, *"Lord I am not worthy for you to come under my roof..."*. It is a striking note of humility for a man in such a position as he, who is use to giving orders, not being given orders. But he is now ready to receive whatever Jesus tells him.

The Centurion recognized the inherent nature of authority; he himself under authority and having authority over others. And if it's escaped our notice, Jesus too was a man under authority, that of his Father's. Just not in a harsh, servile way, but in a loving, relational, and nurturing way, as a boy to his dad, always watching and listening for his father's directions and instructions.

Jesus gasped at the depth of the Centurion's understanding and faith, and say's so: *"He marveled!"* And said to the crowd, *"Truly I have never seen such a great faith in anyone of Israel."* That is a remarkable statement, as this kind of faith was unheard of among Gentiles, he couldn't even find it among his Jewish countrymen!

Jesus goes on to make another astounding statement in the hearing of all who were present, that because of this man's understanding of authority, this Gentile's profound insight of faith, and his complete trust in Jesus,[98] that

---

[98] On "believing" see, Mark 9:23; Matt 9:28; 21:22; Mark 5:36; 9:23-24; 11:23-24.

for him to merely say the word and it was as good as done due to the authority he carries.

And it was; *"the servant was healed that very moment"* (v.13b).

This is the *hour* Jesus spoke of with the Samaritan woman when the *"true worshippers"* whom the Father seeks would gather around Him in *"spirit and reality."* They were witnessing that very *hour*, and the day would come when women (like the Samaritan), and men (like this Gentile Roman Centurion) would be invited to recline at the table of the Lord and dine with Abraham, Isaac and Jacob in the kingdom of heaven. This while the very *"sons of the kingdom would be cast out into outer darkness, where there will be weeping and gnashing of teeth"* (Matt. 8:11-13).

At the future Messianic banquet[99] those who gather together *"from east and west"* will be of genuine faith to sit with the Father as His own sons and daughters bearing the very image of the Lord Jesus to experience the joy of face-to-face koinonia (fellowship) with Him at His family table.

"Do not fear, for I am with you; I will bring your offspring

from the east, and gather you from the west. I will say to

---

[99] Revelation 19:9.

the north, 'Give them up!" And to the south, "Do not hold

them back." Bring my sons from afar and my daughters

from the ends of the earth, everyone who is called by

My Name, and whom I have created for my glory, whom

I have formed, even whom I have made" (Isaiah 43:5-7).

"Worthy are you, our Lord and our God, to receive glory and

honor and power; for you created all things, and because of

Your will they existed, and were created" (Revelation 4:11).

What we do now in eating the Lord's supper is something like a dress rehearsal to the wedding that takes place in the celestial kingdom at the Lord's return for his beautiful bride. On that day there will be a celebratory banquet where we will recline at the table of the Lord;

"Blessed are those who are invited to the marriage supper of the Lamb" ... *"Be like men who are waiting for their master when he returns from the wedding feast, so that they may immediately open the door when he comes and knocks. Blessed are those slaves whom the master will find on the alert when he comes; truly I say to you, that he will gird himself to serve, and have them*

recline at the table, and will come up and wait on them" (Rev. 19:9; Luke 12:36-37; Rev. 21-22).

Partaking of Divine Life

Another text greatly misunderstood is John 6,[100] especially among the Sacramentalists. It is violently wrenched out of its contextual setting and shoehorned into meaning the Lord's supper, by which they mean the sacrament of the "eucharist." Many evangelicals too misunderstand this text and make the same mistake associating it with the Lord's supper.

This section begins with the miracle of feeding some five thousand people with five fish and two loaves of barley bread near the Passover season (v.4). And they ate *"as much as they wanted,"* and were *"filled"* (Jn. 6:11-13), with 12 baskets of leftovers![101] He exceeded what they needed.

This section reminds me of the old adage that says: *"He has done so much for so long with so little, He's now qualified to do anything with nothing."*

Right on the heels of this miracle Jesus walks on the sea of Galilee in the midst of a violent storm about three or four miles out. He invites Peter out of the boat to join him but ends up needing to be rescued. And when they

---

[100] John's account is also recorded in Matt. 14:13-23; Mk. 6:30-46; Lk. 9:10-17.

[101] 2-fish, 5-barley loaves=7 total. 12 baskets of leftovers, one for each of the 12 apostles to serve the departing crowd so that nothing was wasted of God's inexhaustible abundance.

join the others in the boat, immediately the storm ceased, and the next thing they knew they were ashore.

They were completely befuddled, utterly confused, and confounded beyond words on how to comprehend this. Why? Because they had gained no insight from the miracle of feeding the five thousand with the barley loaves, because their hearts and minds were still in the dark as to Jesus' true identity (Mark 6:51-52), and what God was accomplishing in bringing about the kingdom of heaven right in their very midst in the person of Jesus Christ. This matter of believing was not a matter of inability but of unwillingness.

The significance in the sequence of events immediately coupled to the storm story which the twelve all personally witnessed and participated in should have given them greater insight into the identity of Jesus, far beyond what the crowds had witnessed who the twelve had just served but apparently it did little to advance their apprehension as to his true identity.

Recall that after miraculously feeding that horde of people they intended to take Jesus by force and make him king. But he *perceived* this and so secretly slipped away to be alone in the mountains that overlooked the area and the sea, Jn. 6:15-25.

Jesus had miraculously fed them and miraculously rescued them from the storm.

Once the crowds caught up with him again Jesus exposed their motivation for seeking him, which was completely worldly and carnal; they wanted an earthly king and wanted their stomachs filled (vv. 15, 26). And they were going to great lengths, working to achieve those ends; *"Do not work for the food which perishes but for the food which endures to eternal life, which the Son of Man will give you, for on him the Father, God has set His seal"* [102] (vv.22-25, 27).

If we adopt this same carnal attitude as these Jews, ingrained as they were into thinking the kingdom of God was geo-political, and that God wants us to be doing some kind of work to earn salvation and retain His favor we too will have missed the boat.

They had not worked for the bread and fish Jesus had just fed them with and neither did the children of Israel work for the bread that fell from heaven in the wilderness during the days of Moses. Both were freely given and both perish with the eating. In contrast the food God offers is spiritual, imperishable and endures to life eternal, and that is the life Jesus is offering them to *partake*[103] of, not the eating of food, but the eating of himself by faith, which again is spiritual. It is to *partake of His nature,* to live by His indwelling life, absorb His character, and display His image in the world.

---

[102] The "seal" is a reference to the voice of God from heaven at his baptism when the dove descended upon him, Matt 3:16-17, and also to the signs and wonders he performed that followed, Jn. 5:17-19; Mark 6:1-6.

[103] II Peter 1:4, *"...He has granted to us His precious and magnificent promises, so that by them we become partakers of the divine nature…".*

Neither the Lord's supper for the evangelical, or the transubstantiated host for the Catholic are in view here. It is a profound misunderstanding to interpret what Jesus is speaking of here as some sort of Lord's supper. Just as Nicodemus misunderstood the meaning of the new birth as some sort of literal physical birth,[104] which was not at all what Jesus was speaking about.

They then asked Jesus, "What work shall we do that are the works of God?" (v.28).

What is the **work**? Believe! "Believe in him whom He has sent" (v.29). The Lord is being ironic in his reply, belief is not a work in a physical sense. It is a greater spiritual discernment and apprehension the Lord is bringing them into, a spiritual apprehension not of works of the law, nor of intellect, or eating physical food, but of spiritual life. Which is how Jesus lived (6:15), not by *fallen* unperceptive human intellect, human will power, or human emotion.

Jesus lived by his Father's life; "As the living Father sent me, and I live _by_ the Father, so he who eats me, he also will live _by_ me" (v.58, my emphasis).

First, Jesus corrects their misunderstanding, it was not Moses who gave them the bread form heaven, but "my Father" (v.32).[105] And now He is giving them the true

---

[104] See, John 3:1-15, Jesus speaks of a new spiritual birth, per Jn. 1:12-13.
[105] See, Exodus 16:4; Psalms 78:24, the food of angels.

bread out of heaven, and this bread gives eternal life to the world (v.33).

Like the Samaritan woman at the well of Jacob who wanted the water Jesus was offering her so that she would never thirst again, or have to come all the way out to the well in order to draw water (John 4:10-15), they too wanted this bread; *"Lord, always give us this bread"* (v.34).

V.35 is the first of seven *"I am"* statements by Jesus.[106] Two synonymous parallel statements are made by Jesus after he announces *"I am the bread of life"*;

   a) Come to Me … Hunger Not
   b) Believes in Me … Thirst Not

Vv.36-40, Jesus charged, *"they had seen, yet not believed."* A clear refusal of faith.

His coming down was to lose none whom the Father had given him and raise them up (past, present, and future) on the *"last day"* (vv.39-40, 44).

Recall the Wilderness Wanderings

Vv.41-43, *"Grumbling"* at God's messenger (Ex. 15:24; 16:2)

---

[106] The seven *"I Am"* statements are linked to Ex. 3:14; Jn. 6:35; 8:12; 10:7, 11; 11:25; 14:6; 15:1.

The water (Ex. 15:24; 17:1-3)[107]

The bread or *"manna"* from heaven (Num. 11:4-6)

Even the flesh, meat of the quail that fell from heaven (Num. 11:31-33)

They are still *"grumbling"* at God, rejecting His messenger and His provision; *"I am the bread that came down out of heaven"* (v.41).

Jn. 6:45, Jesus fulfills Isaiah 54:13, *"They shall be taught of God."* Because only those who are drawn by the Father will come to Jesus to *"hear"* and *"learn"* from the Father.

God inspires faith in the spirit of man to believe what he cannot of himself understand, due to the deadness of his spirit, yet cannot deny what he has seen and experienced. God does not give us our faith[108] but He is certainly in it as He draws us to Him in His Son. The appeal is to receive the word and believe in order to gain divine life.

To repeat; *"coming to"* and *"believing in"* are the same as *"eating"* and *"drinking."* Just as eating and drinking sustains physical life, so too does *coming to* and *believing in* sustain our spiritual life.

---

[107] See also, Psalms 81:7b-16.
[108] See, Romans 10:17; Ephesians 2:8—faith to believe.

V.49, Israel ate the bread from heaven in the wilderness and died.

Vv.50-51, but to eat the bread of heaven who is God incarnate in the Lord Jesus Christ is to live eternally. How? By *"believing."*

Earlier Jesus had chided the unbelieving Jews, *"Unless you people see signs and wonders, you simply will not believe"* (Jn. 4:48). This same attitude describes many today but especially the Sacramentalist who emphasize the need for the bread to be literally turned into the physical flesh of Jesus in the performance of the ceremonial Mass by the Roman priest by the miracle of "transubstantiation."

Even though the Catholic Mass is supposedly a reenactment of the brutal death of Christ on the cross they still call it a "celebration."[109] There is no greater contradiction in all of Scripture than to say as Catholicism does, they make present the dying of Christ on the cross in each and every Mass, and without it salvation cannot be renewed to the parishioner by the Roman Church.

The context of Hebrews 9:23-28 shows us conclusively the utter uselessness and futility of a Catholic Mass which they claim is the re-sacrifice of Christ on the cross. We read;

---

[109] As do many evangelicals even though they set-in stone-cold silence through their Lord's suppers too.

"Therefore, it was necessary for the copies of the things in the heavens to be cleansed with these, but the heavenly things themselves with better sacrifices than these. For Christ did not enter a holy place made with hands, a mere copy of the true one, but into heaven itself, now to appear in the presence of God for us; nor was it that He would offer Himself often, as the high priest enters the holy place year by year with blood that is not his own. Otherwise, He would have needed to suffer often since the foundation of the world; but now once at the consummation of the ages He has been manifested to put away sin by the sacrifice of Himself. And inasmuch as it is appointed for men to die once and after this comes judgment, so Christ also, having been offered once to bear the sins of many, will appear a second time for salvation without reference to sin, to those who eagerly await Him" (NASB, emphasis mine. Notice the contrasts between often and once).

Furthermore, Hebrews 10 goes on to tell us that the one-time sacrifice of Christ on the cross of Golgotha was in contrast to the Old Covenant sacrifices and the Levitical priests who continually offered them on the temple altar, all of which foreshadowed the Lord's singular, one-time, never-to-be-repeated sacrificial death, which included the Passover lamb that was offered year after year and fulfilled in Christ Jesus. We read;

"For the Law, since it has only a shadow of the good things to come and not the very form of things, can never, by the same sacrifices which they offer continually year by year, make perfect those who draw near. Otherwise, would they not have ceased to be offered, because the worshipers, having once been cleansed, would no longer have had consciousness of sins? But in those sacrifices, there is a <u>reminder</u> of sins year by year. For it is impossible for the blood of bulls and goats to take away sins. Therefore, when He comes into the world, He says,

"Sacrifice and offering You have not desired,

But a body You have prepared for Me; in whole burnt offerings and sacrifices for sin You have taken no pleasure.

"Then I said, 'Behold, I have come (in the scroll of the book it is written of Me) to do Your will, O God.'"

After saying above, "Sacrifices and offerings and whole burnt offerings and sacrifices for sin You have not desired, nor have You taken pleasure in them" (which are offered according to the Law), then He said, "Behold, I have come to do Your will." He takes away the first in order to establish the second. By this will we have been sanctified through the offering of the body of Jesus Christ once for all. Every priest stands daily ministering and offering time after time the same sacrifices, which can never take away sins; but He, having offered <u>one</u> sacrifice for sins for all time, 'Sat down at the right hand of God,' waiting from that time onward 'Until His enemies be made a footstool for His feet.' For by one offering He has perfected for all time those who are sanctified. And the Holy Spirit also testifies to us; for after saying,

"This is the covenant that I will make with them after those days, says the Lord: I will put My laws upon their heart, and on their mind I will write them." He then says, "And their sins and their lawless deeds <u>I will remember no more.</u>" Now where there is forgiveness of these things, there is <u>no longer any offering</u> for sin" (NASB, vv.1-18, emphasis mine).

Our Lord ended all of that *"once and for all"*! (Heb. 10:10). His sacrificial death on the cross needs no addition, which includes the repetitive sacrifice of Christ Himself being reenacted in the Catholic Mass time and time again. And by inferior priests!

These two chapters in Hebrews stand in stark contrast to the Catholic dogma of the sacrificial Mass, transubstantiation, the altar table and the entire priesthood of the Roman Catholic Church.

Hebrews 10:18 emphatically states, *"where there is forgiveness of these things, there is no longer any offering for sin."* Let's restate that in the negative; *"where there is no forgiveness of these things, there must be a continual offering for sin."* That is what the Roman Church says it is doing in the Mass, because Christ's one time sacrifice for all was not sufficient. They have reverted to the old covenant system of repeated sacrifices!

Our Lord Jesus Christ is now seated at the right hand of the Father (10:12) in the heavens because his all-sufficient work of atonement for sins is finished. To say that it is not and continue to reenact that sacrificial death in the Mass as the Catholic priest pretends to do is to invite the wrath of God: "*How much severer punishment do you think he will deserve who has trampled underfoot the Son of God, regarding as unclean* (insufficient) *the blood of the covenant by which he was sanctified, and has insulted the Spirit of grace?*" (Heb. 10:29). There cannot possibly be anything added to the one time, once for all sacrifice of Christ by anyone that could possibly touch the cross of glory!

He who is the Living Bread is also the Lamb of God who is sacrificed for the sins of the world (11:50-52; 17:19). As the Baptist said, "*Behold the lamb of God who is to take away the sins of the world!*" (Jn. 1:29).

The emphasis is not on Christ's death for sin, but on his death for life, "*And I, if I am lifted up from the earth, will draw all men to myself*" (Jn. 12:32; 3:14). By his crucifixion Jesus is offering his flesh for the life of the world (Jn. 6:51c). It is the same as saying that he would "*give his life a ransom for the many*" (Mk. 10:45).

His death redeemed our soul, our spirit, and in the "*last day*" our own flesh.[110]

Jn. 6:35, 40, 50-51 increasingly intensify the image of eating (and drinking) the Bread of Life, but again the

---

[110] Man was created a living soul (Gen. 2:7); mind, will, emotion. Ezek. 18:4, *"The soul that sins will die."* Sin resulted in spiritual death, and eventually physical death. Redemption in Christ reverses spiritual death and brings the soul into balance and lastly our fleshly body is resurrected to life eternal; I Cor. 15:42-46, *"'The first man Adam became a living soul.' The last Adam became a life-giving spirit."*

Lord's supper is not in view here as if the "elements" in themselves contain eternal life so that eating them imparts life to you, which is the view of Roman Catholicism. There is nothing intrinsic to bread and wine that contain eternal life in themselves, nor can any man add this to them. Only Christ Jesus has life in himself (Jn. 5:21, 26; Col. 2:9),[111]and as we have pointed out, he shares his life with those who hear and believe (Jn. 6:29). Acceptability to God is not performance based, it is belief based.

There is a striking difference between the "spiritual Christian" and the "carnal Christian" —and yes, these two breeds still exist within the species. The "carnally minded Christian" is who the Apostle Paul is speaking of in I Cor. 5:11; he is the "so-called brother" who is living immorally. Again, these still exist but rarely are they found in or among an organic habitat of a body of believers, but are ubiquitous among institutional churches, shamefully they are not only tolerated but even promoted.

At this point in his ministry Jesus[112] begins to winnow out the carnally minded seekers form the spiritually minded seekers; the wheat from the chaff; the heavenly from the earthly.

His announcement that he is the bread of life, that his flesh is real food was a difficult statement, many

---

[111] Jn. 5:26, the Father, Son and Holy Spirit who comprise the godhead are uncreated life, the highest life.
[112] Entering his 3rd year of ministry.

stumbled at this teaching and withdrew from following him (v.52, 60, 66).

The NEB translates Jn. 6:60 as, *"This is more than we can stomach! Why listen to such talk!?"* What we today would say, *"That's crazy talk!"*

All four Gospels record the feeding of the 5,000, three of which immediately follow with the Lord walking on the sea of Galilee and calming the storm, Luke's account is a bit different; Matt. 14:13-33; Mk. 6:31-52; Lk. 9:10-17 (8:22-25); Jn. 6:1-21. It's obvious from the narrative that the "feeding event" was intended to teach his disciples a vital lesson about his true identity, that he was far more than just a miracle working prophet (Jn. 6:14; Lk. 9:18-19). The twelve should have especially gotten this lesson because right on the heels of feeding over 5,000 people they witnessed him walking on the water in the midst of the storm and calming the sea. But again, they seem to have gained little to no insight into Jesus' true identity.

The NEB[113] renders Mk. 6:50-52 as; *"Their hearts were hardened."*

NLT; *"Their hearts were to hard to take it in."*

NAS; *"...for they had not gained any insight from the incident of the loaves, but their heart was hardened."*

---

[113] New English Bible, New Living Translation, New American Standard.

Incredibly, their spirits still lay in darkness to perceive the true identity of their Lord.

Bread rained down from heaven on their ancestors in the wilderness (Ex. 16:13-36; Num. 11:4-9), which sustained their mortal lives. Now bread from heaven once again had rained down upon the children of Israel in the wilderness, but *this bread* would sustain their immortal lives. This bread is the incarnate Word of God.

A Time of Turmoil

Both Numbers 11, and John 6 were a time of turmoil for the children of Israel who'd become sick of the bread from heaven,[114] and complained bitterly to God and His chosen one in Moses. We read; *"but now our appetite is gone. There is nothing at all to look at except this manna"* (v.6). Incredibly they longed for the provisions of Egypt (v.5), from where they had just been rescued. So, God miraculously provided bread from heaven followed by *"flesh"* that also rained down from heaven in the *"quail"* when the people complained saying; *"who will give us flesh to eat."* Throughout Numbers 11 the Hebrew word for *"flesh"* is translated as *"meat"* in our English Bibles (See verses 4, 13-2x's, 18-3x's, 21, 23).

This is obviously what Jesus is referring to when He speaks of giving His flesh to eat. He is comparing it to the quail God miraculously and providentially provided to

---

[114] See also Numbers 21:5, where again they complained about the bread form heaven.

Israel which fell from the heavens, see Num. 11:18-21; 31-35.[115]

This was a well-known event in Israel's history yet they failed to recognize the significance of it as being fulfilled in Jesus.

Just as the Samaritan woman said to Jesus at the well of Jacob when told of living water; *"Sir, give me this water, that I may not thirst..."* (Jn. 4:15). These Galileans too said of the life-giving bread; *"Sir, give us this bread always"* (Jn. 6:34). But concerning His flesh—they loathed, Num. 11:20; Jn. 6:60.

I do not think we need to point out that our Lord was not speaking to the Samaritan woman about drinking real, physical H2O water, even though that is how she at first took the meaning. And neither was the Lord speaking to these Galileans about eating real, physical flesh, even though that is how they understood him.[116]

Was there anyone more misunderstood than our Lord Jesus in what he taught?!

Next Jesus would say, *"Truly, truly, I say to you, I am the door of the sheep"* (Jn. 10:7). Did anyone take that literally? That he was literally a real door, a physical

_____

[115] See also Psalms 78:23-30 where both the bread and meat are linked together.

[116]Nicodemus too misunderstood the Lord when speaking of a second birth, Jn. 3:1-12. And Jesus chided him for his ignorance, v.10. The inexcusable ignorance of Nicodemus stands in contrasted to the Samaritan woman's understandable misunderstanding.

gate? **No**. John even gives us a footnote in v.6, that this was *"a figure of speech Jesus spoke to them"* and they still did not understand what he was saying.

Jesus is a figure in all of these;

~Jesus is the living water of whom we drink and never thirst again.

~Jesus is the bread that we eat and never hunger again.

~Jesus is the gate by which we enter and never stray again.

Jesus alone is the complete diet of the believer in eating and drinking for spiritual sustenance for the spiritual man and woman of God. Just as He is the *Way*, the *Truth* and the *Life* (Jn. 14:6).

Only by willful ignorance, or having been mistaught will a person come away thinking that bread and water mean something physical and literal. We may indeed be guilty of misunderstanding him, but we may safely conclude, it is not Jesus doing the misteaching. We need only be willing to listen and hear him; *"If anyone is willing to do his will, he will know of the teaching, whether it is of God or whether I speak from myself"* (Jn. 7:17).

It's obvious from their response they were extremely offended by the idea of eating the flesh of Jesus and drinking his blood, which is something flatly condemned by Jewish Law (Leviticus 7:26-27; 17:10-14; 19:26; Deut. 12:23, which speaks of animals, to say nothing of human flesh and blood), and was utterly repulsive to the law keeping "kosher" Jew. It amounts to cannibalism if taken literally.

John 6:52, the Jews say in response to Jesus' words of eating his flesh; *"How can this man give us his flesh to eat?"* Verse 60, *"Therefore many disciples, when they heard this said, 'This is a difficult statement; who can listen to it?'"* And v.66; *"As a result of this, many of His disciples withdrew and were not walking with Him anymore."* Seemingly all but the twelve left him, vv.67-69.

But Jesus answered their objection to clear up this misunderstanding, *"It is the Spirit who gives life, the flesh profits nothing"* (*"flesh...is no help at all"*, ESV; *"the flesh counts for nothing"*, NIV); *"the words that I have spoken to you are spirit and are life"* (Jn. 6:63). Clearly the literal meaning of *"eat my flesh"* is ruled out by his answer and those carnally minded are winnowed away so that all who remain will come to see the spiritual meaning.

Even now with the benefit of 20/20 hind-sight and the complete context of not only the Gospels, but the Acts, all the epistles, and the Old Testament types and shadows (which by design move us from outer forms to inner realities; from the physical to the spiritual), we ask; how can anyone take his words to "eat my flesh and drink my blood" literally? Obviously, there is a hidden meaning, a spiritual meaning to his words.

Nevertheless, this is how the Roman Catholic Church insists it is to be interpreted. Even though in this very context Jesus plainly stated, *"the flesh profits nothing"*, that the *"words I have spoken are spirit and are life"* (v.63)—meaning there is a spiritual meaning!

The spiritual meaning of his words are hidden form the carnally minded. They must be appraised by the spiritually minded, those who combine *"spiritual thoughts with spiritual words."*[117] It is *"hidden manna"*[118] the Lord is offering and can only be consumed by a man's spirit within him where he is nourished on the things of God, who hears the Spirit with spiritual ears.

What the Roman Church say's is akin to what the *"Rabble"* (the *"mixed multitude"*) said coming out of Egypt that caused the sons of Israel to stumble along with them; *"Who will give us flesh to eat?"*[119] Discontent with what God Almighty had done to bring them out of the cruel bondage and misery of Egypt, they now *lusted*, and even *wept* in their carnal desires for what lay behind them[120] and expressed their contempt for God's provisions with, *"There is nothing at all to look at except this manna"* (Numbers 11:6).

Their deadened spiritual sensibilities, like Israel's of old, had hardened their hearts[121] to the spiritual realities

---

[117] See, I Cor. 2:13-14.
[118] See, Rev. 2:17.
[119] See, Num. 11:4, KJV, et, al.; (Lk. 9:62). *"Flesh to eat"* is used eight times in this chapter alone.
[120] See, Num. 11:4-5, fish, cucumbers, melons, leeks, onions, garlic. Ex. 16:3, *"the flesh pots"* of Egypt.
[121] See, Mark 6:50-52, the parallel to this event in John's Gospel.

Jesus was attempting to lead them into. They said, "*...who can listen to it?*" (Jn. 6:60c).

This prompted Jesus to ask them, "*Does this cause you to stumble?*"[122] (Jn. 6:61b). Undoubtedly the Lord marveled at their hardness of heart given all that they had seen and heard from him, and given the language of prophets like Ezekiel, who was God's man to speak to the children of Israel; "*Now you, son of man, listen to what I am speaking to you; do not be rebellious like that rebellious house. Open your mouth and eat what I am giving to you*" (Ezek. 2:8-3:11).

Ezekiel was fed a scroll, which "*was as sweet as honey in my mouth*"—truth discovered is always sweet. But as soon as we begin to act on it and live it out, it can be quite bitter; "*I was in bitterness, in the heart of my spirit*" (Ezek. 2:14, KJV).

Why the bitterness after consuming the sweet? Because he then went on to declare God's message to a hard hearted, hard of hearing, rejecting people just as did Jesus. The very people who should have been the most receptive to God's word turned out to be the least receptive and downright hostile to God's messenger, and consequently His message.

The same thing happened with the apostle John on the island of Patmos who was given to write Revelation, an Angel gave him a scroll to eat; "*and in my mouth it was as sweet as honey; and when I had eaten it, my stomach was*

---

[122] Some versions render *"stumble"* as *"offend."*

made bitter" (Rev. 10:9-10). When we ingest the Gospel of Christ it is as sweet as honey because it imparts Christ to us. But when we digest it, we are often met with bitter rejection and sorrow by those who refuse God's message of salvation in Christ, and we who proclaim it are rejected as well.

The descriptive verbiage Jesus was using here with these Synagogue attending Jews should not have been out of their depth[123] to catch his meaning. It was typical of the descriptive, illustrative, figurative, even apocalyptic language read from the Law and prophets every Sabbath. Yet the word's Jesus spoke about eating his flesh and drinking his blood came across to them as a foreign language.

The very One who is life incarnate now stands as an "offense" to them!? His own creation who bear his image. The humility of our Lord Jesus is peerless and unfathomable.

Let's Review

The Hidden Manna foreshadows our meal with God. It is the messianic banquet at the consummation of the age, the marriage supper of the Lamb when his sons and daughters gather around the table of our Father (Matt. 8:10-12; 22:2-14; Lk. 14:15-24; 22:28-30; Rev. 2:17; 19:7-9).

---

[123] See, "The Hard Sayings of Jesus" by F.F. Bruce, 1983, Chap. 1.

The manna is a symbol of Jesus himself who is the *bread of life*. Manna is the food from heaven, the *"food of angels"*—it is Christ himself come down from heaven. He is not only the food of angels in the heavenlies, but also the food of humanity on the earth; both angels and men live by His life. He unites both realms in himself; hidden in the heavens, revealed in the earth so that both humanity and angels are united as the sons of God in both realms; God's seen and unseen sons are united in Him in fellowship (Ps. 78:24-25; 105:40; Job 38:7; Rom. 8:14; Rev. 3:20; 22:17).

Jesus as the *"Bread of Life"* isn't just a once-a-week occurrence of the Lord's supper,[124] our Lord is an everyday Bread like that which fell from heaven with the morning dew in order to provide the children of Israel their daily portion (Ex. 16:4-5; Num. 11:9; Deut. 8:3, 16).

In short, to interpret John 6 to mean eating the Lord's supper is to relegate the Bread of Life to just a once-a-week ceremony, or ordinance. Is it not for this very reason the Lord said, *"...the words that I have spoken to you are spirit and are life"* (Jn. 6:63b)? This is said to arrest a purely fleshly pursuit; spirit and life are in opposition to flesh and death.

Consider too, the words of the apostle that *"the righteousness based on faith speaks as follows: 'Do not say in your heart, 'Who will ascend into the heavens?' (That is to bring Christ down), or 'Who will descend into*

---

[124] But that's all He can be for the fundamentalist Christian who interpret Jn. 6 as being the Lord's supper.

the abyss?' (That is, to bring Christ up from the dead)'" (Rom. 10:6-7). Yet that is exactly what the Roman Church says it does during the ritual of "transubstantiation"; they bring Christ up from the dead and down from heaven as they turn the bread into his flesh and the wine into his blood in the performance of the ceremonial/sacrificial/ritualistic Mass.

Paul is citing Deuteronomy 30:11-14, with an appeal to Deut. 8:17 and 9:4.[125] Israel was

clearly instructed as to what was required of them and it was not too difficult to obey, nor was it out of reach. You won't have to ascend into heaven to get it, and you won't have to descend into death (symbolic of going back beyond the Red Sea, the Abyss) to get it.

How close is it? As close as your own breath; *"But the word is very near you, in your mouth and in your heart, that you may observe it"* (Deut. 30:14). It is by your own breath that you may call upon the name of the Lord, and His name is His presence, they are inextricably linked together (I Cor. 12:3b).

In sum: It's really all about what God has done, is doing, and is going to do. It's not about what you've done, can do, or will do. Except one thing, the only thing you can do, and it is all that is required of you; *"believe."* Remember who has delivered you, led you, provided for you, and has

---

[125] Deuteronomy chat's. 8 and 9 are an appeal to Israel not to forget or become arrogant toward God Almighty who has deliver you from Egypt and secured the promise land of Canaan on your behalf.

conquered for you. Observe what He has said and place your faith, your trust, and complete confidence in Him.

Paul's conclusion in Romans 10; *"But what does it say? 'The word is near you, in your mouth and in your heart'— that is the word of faith which we are preaching..."* (vv.8-10, 13).

We do not need a "Mass" officiated (to bring Christ down), and bread "transformed" (to bring Christ up) by a Roman priest in order to consume our Lord. We need only take Him into our hearts by faith, and confess His name with our lips because our words and our mouth are directly connected to our spirit by our breath.[126]

Real Bread is a He, not an it. He came down from heaven as eatable bread (Jn. 6:32-38).

Remember, *"the flesh profits nothing"*[127] Jesus said. So, it is not by eating something physical, it is by eating someone spiritual.

The mouth confesses what the heart believes. The heart is the spiritual organ that takes in Christ who is life and spirit and whosoever eats of His life will have the same life He has in him, or her, and will be able to live by that

---

[126] Hebrew wd. "ru'ah" for spirit is the same for breath, air, wind, etc. See Ps. 33:6; Judges 15:19; II Kings 10:4-5. And God has given us the breath of life, Gen. 2:7.
[127] As Jesus said, Jn. 6:63b.

life (Jn. 6:57, 63a).[128] It is created life partaking of Uncreated life, human life partaking of Divine life.

Our Lord is not speaking of physical food or physical drink in John 6, He is speaking of partaking of His spirit which imparts eternal life; *"It is the Spirit who gives life...the words I have spoken to you are spirit and life"* (Jn. 6:61a, c).

When Jesus spoke of spirit, He spoke of life. And when He spoke of life He spoke of spirit. He is spirit and is life, and the believer can live by His Spirit and His Life when he or she partakes of Him by faith. Confessing Him with our mouth, and believing in Him with our heart results in *"righteousness"* (Rom. 10:10-11); it is just that easy! This is what spiritual eating and drinking is; it is to consume Him by faith, connecting our spirit to His by means of faith, confessing with our mouth *"Jesus as Lord."* Not by eating transformed bread, but by eating Christ Jesus who transforms us. And that is what conversion is; transformation (Rom. 12:1-2).

No man has ever descended from heaven, and no man has ever ascended into heaven whose origins are of that realm, except the Lord Jesus Christ (Jn. 3:13; 7:34). This agrees with Romans 10.

God's eternal purpose is summed up in these several verse of John 6:37-40, and 56-58;

---

[128] See also, Jn. 5:26, 11:25 and II Tim. 1:10 for divine life imparted to human life.

"All that the Father gives me, will come to me, and the one who comes to me I will certainly not cast out. For I have come down from heaven, not to do my own will, but the will of him who sent me. This is the will of Him who sent me, that of all He has given me I lose nothing, but raise it up on the last day. For this is the will of my Father, that everyone who beholds the Son and believes in him will have eternal life, and I myself will raise him up on the last day."

"He who eats my flesh and drinks my blood abides in me, and I in him. As the living Father sent me, and I live by the Father, so he who eats me he also will live by me. This is the bread which came down out of heaven; not as the fathers ate and died; he who eats this bread will live forever."

First, the Lord's promise is to reappropriate, and repurpose a people out of the world to Himself through Christ Jesus who appeals to our spirits which are from God, *"the Father of spirits"* (Heb. 12:9; I Cor. 15:45h; Rev. 11:11; Gen. 2:7; Num. 27:16).[129] It was God's eternal purpose to send the Son for this very purpose, the Son *"knows those that are his."*[130] So that when He speaks our inward man hears, our spirit recognizes His voice and we begin to follow and participate in His life with Him and in the things that He says.

---

[129] This includes both the righteous and the wicked spirits of men.

[130] See, II Tim. 2:19; I Cor. 8:3.

Jesus, in his own words put it this way; *"I am the good shepherd, and I know my own and my own know me"* (Jn. 10:14-15, 27). We recognize his voice and begin to *follow* Him. Calvinists of a Reformed theological persuasion call this "irresistible grace" (due to God's foreknowledge and predestination, if properly understood), and we do not deny God knows those who are His, as Scripture says; *"The Lord knows those who are His"* (II Tim. 2:19). He works within our spirit to draw us to Him. But it is not without our free will participation and response to His inward call.[131] Our spiritual response works in synergy with God's spiritual calling. It is the result of hearing Him, and coming to know[132] the Lord Jesus Christ by experience in an ever-deeper way which can never be fully exhausted. We simply ask; "If grace is irresistible as some claim, what was Judas doing? Not to mention all the Jews who heard and saw the Lord Jesus and flatly resisted him?"[133]

Our point in this is that God gives us free will to respond or reject Him. Just as Adam was invited to eat of the Tree of Life, not of the tree of knowledge of good and evil. This is II Peter 3:9 in a nutshell, the Lord is *"...patient toward you, not wishing for any to perish but*

---

[131] Biblically, there is no mention of irresistible grace. God's grace is constantly resisted. This doctrine was invented by Augustine in the 5th century. See, "What love is this?" by Dave Hunt, 3rd ed., 2006.

[132] "Know" is the Gk. wd. *"ginosko"* by progressive experience of being connected to Him in an active relationship. Matt. 7:23, *"I never knew you"*, i.e., never in an approving connected relationship.

[133] See, Luke 7:29-30 on this point.

for all to come to repentance." God does not override our free will response to grace.

Second, *"seeing"* and *"believing"* in the Son is a transformative event (v.40). What we look upon, are most consciously occupied with we begin to resemble, and are conformed to. This *"seeing"* or *"beholding"* is in the passive voice, meaning it acts on you, you don't act on it, that would be the active voice. You are *transformed* by beholding, not with physical eyes but with spiritual eyes.

This is how Jesus Christ acts on us, as food and drink. A people together who continually invite the Lord into our spiritual dining room to *sup with us,* which is a transformative event, from the inside out. Eating and drinking the Lord changes us spiritually, it is to partake of His spiritual nature by beholding Him, and learning Him with one another.[134]

The experience of eating and drinking our Lord together is what satisfies our spiritual appetite. It is for those who know they are poor in spirit and who hunger and thirst after righteous (Matt. 5:3, 6, et, al.). Our spiritual portion is the Lord Jesus and it is that portion that each one shares of Him with one another in our meetings (I Cor. 14:26).

Occasionally you'll run into those whose spirits are not poor, who lack humility, there is no brokenness, and no self-awareness of their spiritually destitute nature.

---

[134] See, II Cor. 3:7-18, in Moses a veil covered their eye, in Christ the veil is lifted and we behold Him unto transformation.

They turn what is spiritual into something physical, self-promoting, because that's what appeals to them and their soulish appetites. Recognize and discern these people as quickly as possible when they come among you, they are not suited for a genuine expression of God's people.[135]

Such people are better suited for the institutional church (or synagogue), where there are built in guard rails that limit their interaction and the damage they can inflict upon others. Of course, it also limits their spiritual maturity. At least until they crave a fuller diet of Jesus Christ among His people.

Concerning vv.56-58, God's Eternal Purpose

If you were to ask one hundred preachers of the Gospel;

"What is Genesis through Revelation all about?"

99 out of 100 would say something like;

> "It is about the gradual unfolding of God's plan of redemption for mankind. And how we are to fulfill the Great Commission of Matthew 28:18-20."

Close...but that answer is like hitting a single in the bottom of the 9th inning in game seven of the World

---

[135] See, Matt. 18:15-18; I Cor. 14:23-24, counter opposed to Acts 5 of Ananias and Sapphira, and Acts 8 of Simon the magician, aka, Simon Magus.

Series, trailing 15 to 1 with two outs and no-one on base. There's a lot there to make up!

We suggest a more accurate answer to that question is something like;

> "It is about the gradual unfolding of God's eternal purpose to reveal and magnify His beloved Son in both heaven and earth and conform humanity to His image, by His indwelling life. And to give expression of Him in all the earth as His people."[136]

Included in God's eternal purpose is mankind's redemption in Christ Jesus, but that is decidedly not the central theme of God's revelation contained in the Bible. It is only a "single" in our baseball analogy, when what is needed are sixteen consecutive home runs! Can you imagine that?! God's plan of salvation is a mere strand in the eternal rope that stretches between heaven and earth, each strand constitutes but a single means to God's ultimate purpose, which as we have said, is to reveal the absolute centrality and glory of His Son, the Lord Jesus Christ in both the seen and unseen universe.[137]

---

[136] That is a very brief answer to the question, much more could be said in answer to God's eternal purpose. See, "Unto Full Stature" by DeVern Fromke, pub. Sure Foundations, copyright 2001.

[137] That does not mean God has absolutely no interest in what man does, but He is looking to see who has an interest in Him.

~The first answer places my salvation at the center of all God's activity.

~The second answer places Christ Jesus at the center of all God's activity.

In other words, man's salvation is not God's chief concern; "God's plans and purposes are not determined by man's needs," where God serves the interests of man. God's chief concern is to glorify His Son, and the Son to glorify God's vital Fatherhood.[138] These two are the dominate themes that run throughout the entire Bible, which places God central to all things and man's chief concern is to learn, and to know Him in an experiential way.[139]

Side Note: Count how many sermons, or lessons you've ever heard that deal with God's eternal purpose from eternity to eternity and that are centered entirely on the divine fellowship and the universal Lordship of Jesus Christ...? Then count how many sermons you've heard that are centered on man's salvation and his moral betterment...? Ninety-nine-point-nine percent of all sermons you'll ever hear deal in one way or another with you as the center of God's attention.

---

[138] See, "Ultimate Intention" (pg's. 24-25), by DeVern Fromke, (1963)--revised ed. 1998.

[139] A well-worn book entitled, "What the Bible is All About" by Henrietta C. Mears (first ed., 1953, and 1966 edition) was a Billy Graham favorite. She wrote in answer to this question; "The central theme (of the Bible) is salvation through Jesus Christ" pg. 1.

So, it is in the words of Jesus that *"he who eats my flesh and drinks my blood"*[140]—which is present tense, an activity of abiding in him just as he presently abides in the life of His Father. *"I live by the Father"* because He is eating and drinking the Father of Life. In the same way *"he also will live by Me."* How? By eating and drinking Him, v.57. Just as the Son lived by the Father's life, we now live by the life of the Son. It is similar to the metaphor in Jn. 15:1-6, as a branch is attached to the vine drawing its life from the vine. Upon Him we are centered, to Him we are connected.

Fellowship is spiritual connectedness and spiritual togetherness; *"I and the Father are one"* (Jn. 10:30). Fellowship is also the impartation of life (Jn. 5:26; 11:25-26).

This is the Father's central concern and a brief summary of His eternal purpose; to know His Son (which is to know the Father, Jn 14:8-11; Philippians 3:10) and to live by His indwelling life in a continuously sustained intimate relationship of fellowship with the Lord Jesus Christ (v.58).

This is why we said earlier that the "Lord's supper" is not in view here, or some sort of "eucharistic sacrament," because what the Lord said started right then and there (which is precisely why they were offended). The action was to "believe" in him which was equated to "eating and

---

[140] V.56, aorist tense, is an active present tense verb; "to consume." Same tense in vv.51, 53-54.

drinking him." The language of John 6 is present tense active, and the only way of doing that was in a spiritual sense **not** in a physical sense of literally "munching" on the fleshly body of Jesus, or a symbolic representation of Him. Otherwise, we would have to wait until the next serving of the "transubstantiated eucharist," or the unleavened bread of the Lord's supper before we could eat of Him again.

There is an intimate connection between our physical health and the physical food that we eat, just as there is a spiritual connection between our spiritual health and the spiritual food that we eat. *"We are what we eat"*—both physically and spiritually.

To that point Jesus said, *"...the flesh profits nothing; the words I have spoken to you are spirit and are life"* (Jn. 6:63). So, it is not about eating something physical, consuming skin, meat, flesh. It is about eating/ingesting his words that are spirit. And the only way this eating is done is by faith. Because *"it is the Spirit who gives life"*—again, by faith (v.63a).

Earlier John wrote, *"as many as come to him, to them he gave the right to become children of God, even to those who believe in his name"* (Jn. 1:12). Furthermore, he wrote that those who came to Jesus in belief were *"born, not of blood nor of the will of the flesh nor of man, but of God"* (v.13). That is, you are not born into the family of God's through human reproduction, but by spiritual reproduction; *"after its kind."*[141] You are not *"born again"* through natural man-made means, but supernatural divine means (Jn. 3:4-6). *"The flesh profits nothing"* toward our spiritual birth. It is not accomplished by fleshly means.

"But there are some of you who do not believe" (v.64a). Despite having seen the miracles of Jesus they simply refused to believe in Him as the *"Holy One of God."* In this very context their present tense disbelief is a refusal to *"eat and drink"* of Jesus Christ.

This is how the Father *draws* us to the Son, through His words, which are *"Spirit and life"* (v.63b). And because the Son *knows* the Father and shares His life, the Father reveals to the Son those who do not believe. (Including Judas Iscariot of the twelve, v.71; cf., I Jn. 2:18-27; 3:7-10; 4:1-6).

By this time[142] the twelve had come to believe Jesus was the *"Holy One of God"*—v.69 (which is perfect tense, i.e., "presently happening"). With one exception as noted above, who although he remained among the twelve, he did not completely consent with Peter's next statement, and was to be rightly number among those disciples who deserted the Lord (whatever the reason) and followed Him no more, v.66.

---

[141] See Genesis 1, bearing fruit after its kind is not just physical, but also spiritual in nature.

[142] Jesus said this in the Capernaum Synagogue a short time after feeding the 5,000 and calming the sea.

It is interesting to note that when Simon Peter spoke up on behalf of the twelve, he said, "*You have the words of eternal life*" (v.68b). Peter and the others finally understood the meaning of the Lord's words which imparted life, which are the same as eating and drinking Him, and they did not *stumble* and were not *offended* (v.61), even though they didn't completely understand Him.

In fact, directly related to this is Jesus' next statement to them in v.62; that if they could not understand what it meant to eat his flesh and drink his blood how would they ever understand what it meant to actually see Him "*ascending to where He was before?*" Which is a reference to His ascension to the right hand of God. See, Luke 24:48-52; Acts 1:9-11, and Revelation 5 for a description of His ascension from a heavenly point of view and John's weeping for lack of understanding.

Jesus has already made several statements (and would again) about His death, His resurrection and ascension. See, Jn. 3:13-14; 6:44; 8:21, 28; 12:32; 16:10; 17:11; 20:17; Matt. 16:21; 26:31-32.

"*What then if you see the Son of Man ascending to where He was before?*"

So, if His being the bread of life coming down out of heaven was so difficult to grasp, so incomprehensible, and so offensive to them that they too stumbled and fell away, how would they ever spiritually discern His death, resurrection and ascension back to the Father from where He came?[143] Only the apostle John witnessed that, what took place in the heavenly realm beyond the clouds of earth (Acts 1:9-11; Luke 24:50-51; Mark 16:19), and still, almost sixty years after it happened, he could not comprehend it and wept.

That is until an elder explained to him (what he should have already grasped) that the slain Lamb was actually the Lion of the tribe of Judah, Christ Jesus Himself who has conquered the dragon of sin and death and was worthy to open the book and impart His life!

"*The Lamb slain before the foundation of the world*" (Rev. 13:8).

---

[143] See, John 3:12-13. Of course, the apostle John would years later be given a heavenly view of this ascension event and wrote about it in Revelation 5. We take a late date view of Revelation, written in about 98 AD, vs. an early date of 68 AD.

Chapter 5

Sacramentalism

(A general discussion on the adoption of the sacramental system of pagan Rome)

"The further back you look, the further forward you are likely to see."

—*Winston Churchill*

Sacramentalism encompasses several key aspects of the Roman Church which are essential to its claim of infallibility:

First; religion is a rite[144] that is sacred and public, it cannot be private, a non-public religious rite is viewed as unsanctioned by Sacramentalist thinking and therefore, unauthorized because it is not under the control, or supervision of the Church.

Second; to the Sacramentalist there must be a chain-of-command back to the Church and its authority for any religious rite to have legitimacy.

Third; at the top of the chain-of-command is the pope of Rome who is invested with all authority over the Church (on earth) and ordains all who are under him to

---

[144] Rite and Ritual are interchangeable, is Latin and refers to a religious ceremony or practice.

perform the religious rites of the Church. The pope's authority is derived from an unbroken apostolic succession reaching back to Peter.

It is this third element that is critically essential to the Roman Catholic Church, its entire structure falls apart if this one element is removed. Without it no sacrament of Ordination (i.e., "Holy Orders," the sixth Sacrament of seven, see below) exists, and therefore no religious rites can be performed. Not baptism, not the Mass, not transubstantiation, not the eucharist. Nothing. Why? Because without an ordained Catholic priest to perform and administer these rites they simply cannot be done legitimately. Furthermore, without a pope to do the Ordaining these rites cannot be carried out; hence the entire system falls apart.

The Sacraments belong to the Church, and it is the Sacrament that saves. It is not by personal faith in the Lord Jesus Christ, but the efficacy[145] of the Sacrament that is administered by the Ordained clergy[146] of the Roman Church that saves the sinner. Hence, the Sacraments are what saves the sinner, even when

---

[145] "Efficacy" is not used to describe a person; it describes the devise that brings about a desired result. Namely the "Sacrament" brings to pass an effect. The Sacrament contains inherent power regardless of the character of the person wielding it.

[146] Some of this "touching" of sacred things has changed in just the last 50 to 100 years so that laymen may now touch even the wafer-host without sinning.

passively submitted to as in the baptism of infants, or wearing a Scapular,[147] also a devise with inherent power.

Simply stated, the "Sacraments" are viewed as conferring divine grace and salvation regardless of personal faith and right living.

Rome was a Sacramental religious state long before Jesus Christ came onto the scene. The Sacramental system was inherent in the diverse pagan religions introduced into the Roman empire. It was, in part, because of this unmitigated adoption of all the various and contradictory religions over the centuries, with their opposing values that caused the Roman empire to gradually decline and fall apart, especially when Christianity was injected into its society. Simply because Christianity rendered all other gods and religions, as not just inferior and obsolete (including Judaism), but altogether hostile to the one true faith that is in Jesus Christ. The Roman Catholic Church adopted not only the pre-existing **Sacramental** Roman religious state, but also the hostility that goes with it toward anyone who opposes it.

---

[147] A Scapular (scapula, is Latin for "shoulder blade") is two rectangular pieces of cloth with the image of Mary, or some other Saint embroidered onto it and worn over the shoulders front and back, attached by two stings. If a person dies wearing a Scapular they automatically go to heaven, or at a minimum will not die in the state of mortal sin. At last count, there are 18 different scapulars worn by Catholics today.

The Seven Sacraments of Roman Catholicism are:[148]

1. Baptism
2. Confirmation
3. Holy Communion (the Eucharist)
4. Confession (Penance)
5. Anointing of the Sick (Extreme Unction)
6. Holy Orders (Ordination)
7. Matrimony

In the sacralist system only the ordained priest is qualified to baptize. Baptism is a public rite administered by pouring (effusion) water upon an infant's forehead with witnesses. All other baptisms are unsanctioned and illegitimate, in fact (at one time) they were absolutely forbidden by the Sacramental Church under penalty of death, because they were done by unordained hands.

"Historical knowledge helps put things in context"— *author unknown*. And that is because history, as they say, repeats itself. It simply inserts new faces and new names into a renewed deception. Paganism is religion recycled, it originated in Chaldea (the heart of Babel), which then migrated into Egypt, then Babylon arose, followed by Persia, then Greece, and finally Rome.[149]

In the Roman system of Sacramentalism it is in the ritual of the Mass that Christ is physically made present

---

[148] All seven sacraments serve as props to the Roman system of unity in the Sacramental Church.

[149] See Daniel 2, Nebuchadnezzar's dream of the four-tiered statue and the world kingdoms each one represented.

through the priest's consecration of the bread and wine upon the altar and immolated[150] as an appeasing, propitiatory[151] sacrifice to God. The "unbloody sacrifice" (as it is called) of the circular wafer, is said to be changed into the literal body and blood of Christ, but the Roman Church did not formally adopt this doctrine of the eucharist until 1215 AD at the 4th Lateran Council, and with it, "transubstantiation" as it's official dogma.[152]

In fact, the Roman Church places particular importance on the roundness of the wafer-host, not because there is any biblical teaching on its shape from the O.T. Passover

or the N.T. last supper (which is the fulfillment of the Passover). Quite the opposite, all that the Gospels say is that, *"While they were eating, Jesus took some bread and after a blessing, he broke it and gave it to his disciples, and said, 'Take eat, this is my body...do this in remembrance of me.'"*[153] Is it possible for anything to remain round that is broken?

The "roundness" of the wafer-host is derived from the mystery religions of pagan Egypt, the Chaldeans, the Babylonians, the Greeks and the Romans who worshiped a sun goddess (hence the roundness) who came to be

---

[150] Immolate is "to slay" or "to kill." This is not a word found in the N.T. Bible.

[151] *Propitiation,* "a go between", to reconciled us to God in Christ by his vicarious, expiatory sacrifice, see Heb. 2:17.

[152] See, "The Church of Rome at the Bar of History" by William Webster, 1995.

[153] Ref. to Matt. 26:26; Lk. 22:19. The cup too was drank in remembrance of him.

called "Venus"[154] in Rome and they too considered her the mother goddess of the earth who provided the fruit from her bountiful womb each spring. All of these ancient cultures considered the sun the principal life giver and worshiped her,[155] offering sacrifice to her at sunrise every day. Hence, the round sun-shaped emblem was part of the sacramental mystery religions of pagan Rome that worshiped the sun, and adopted into the Roman Catholic Church in the round wafer-host.

This is particularly illustrated in the Roman Church when the "Monstrance" is used in Processional viewings for the express purpose of the adoration of the wafer-host by parishioners. The Monstrance is shaped[156] like a brilliant sunrise with rays emanating out from all around the center glass called a "luna window" wherein the large round wafer-host is placed. This is called "eucharist adoration" when the wafer-god is put on display during special occasions to be looked upon adoringly.

Another of the many items the Roman priest uses in the performance of the Mass, is the round silver "Paten," a shallow circular saucer that he places the large round wafer-host on. At the moment of "transubstantiation" the wafer-host is lifted up (sometimes with the paten under it to reflect light more brilliantly onto it), as small

---

[154] "The Story of Civilization; Our Oriental Heritage", W. Durant, vol. 4, pg. 235. Cp-writ. 1935, Simon & Schuster.

[155] Egypt's sun goddess was called Isis (among other names); Greeks called her Aphrodite; Rome, Venus. See, "Traditions & Encounters", Jerry Bently & Herb Ziegler, Vol. 1, 3rd ed., 2006.

[156] See web-site: www.pilgrim–info.com/items–used–mass for illustrations and descriptions of utensils used by the Catholic Church.

silver bells are rung at that very moment to signal onlookers to gaze adoringly upon the wafer-host as it is changed into the very body and blood of Christ.

Only by doing the pick and shovel work of research in sifting through the centuries of paganism that Rome willingly adopted from Egypt, Babylon, Greece, etc, which flowed directly into the blood stream of the Roman Catholic Church (especially at the time of Constantine early in the 4th century and thereafter), do we discover how nearly all of Christianity became infected by it.

And it will only be by exercising self-examination and allowing the Spirit of God to penetrate our fallen nature and expose the idolatry of our self-love to our own fallen and deadened spirit so that a genuine revival may begin that knits our spirit back to God.

"Be still, and know that I am God" (Psalms 46:10a, ESV).

Chapter 6

Adopted Paganism

(A general discussion on the introduction of various pagan rituals into Christianity by the fallen-apostate Roman Church)

"He was very intelligent and could name a horse

in seven languages, but rode a cow to work."

—author unknown

As the church progressed from its birth in the early first century, into the early-fourth century it remained home based, persecuted, and held in disdain by the pagan Roman religions throughout the empire. But that all changed when Constantine became the emperor of Rome in 312 AD. He legitimized Christianity and made it the favored state religion of the empire and began to try and unify a tattered and crumbling empire around one universal religion, namely Christianity. The result, over a relatively short period of time, was that pagan Rome became the "Holy Roman Catholic Church."

With that, unconverted pagans poured into the church and quickly changed it into a hierarchical, top-down organizational institution, chalked full of their pagan beliefs and rituals brought in from the pagan shrines and religions that were previously a part of the overall society of the Roman empire.

Never in the history of the world did a culture, an entire civilization exist that had so many gods than the Roman empire. Ancient Roman historian Varro,[157] estimated that there were some 30,000 different deities that had been imported to Rome over the centuries.

Another Roman historian, Petronius[158] remarked that in some towns in Italy there were more gods than men.

Many of these gods represented something sexual in nature;

- ❖ Tutumus, the god of conception.
- ❖ Lucina, the god of menstruation and child birth.
- ❖ Priapus, the god of fertility, which was imported to Rome from Greece.

Both men and women of Rome actually sat on phallic member of this statue to ensure pregnancy. They even wore phallic images of this god's member around their necks to bring about fertility and good luck.

In other words, paganism permeated the entire Roman society. All but the Jews were saturated in polytheism. The typical Roman citizen, or Gentile (of every other nationality and ethnicity other than Jew) was dominated by two entities; the authoritarian State, and the

---

[157] Marcus Terentius Varro, 116-26 B.C. "Caesar and the Christ" Will Duran, vol. 3, pg. 60, 1944, Simon and Schuster, N.Y.
[158] Ibid.

idolatrous pantheon of gods, both foreign and domestic. All of who now resided in the city of Rome.

One historian put it this way; "...when the citizens of a (foreign) community were moved to the capital (Rome) their gods were brought with them...the Romans did not question the existence of these foreign deities, most of them believed that when they led the statue away the god had to come with it; many believed that the statue was the god."[159] Roman Catholicism still operates under this delusion with all its various statues of Mary and the so-called saints as being inhabited by them.

This did not happen overnight of course but little-by-little through a slow progression of centuries. One of the most devastating devices introduced into Christianity from paganism was **"sacerdotalism."** That is, men acting on behalf of God, clothed with His power to whom all others looked for salvation and that the believer does not come directly to God through Jesus Christ, but through the Roman Church and its sacraments.

The "Roman Church" became the mediator of salvation between man and God, via the pope of Rome, who claims to be the head of the Church on earth; the vicar of Christ. And it is he along with his arch-bishops, bishops and ordained priests below them who may intercede to mediate God's grace through the prescribed **"sacraments"** (previously listed).

---

[159] "Caesar and the Christ" Will Durant, vol. 3, pg. 62, pub. 1944, Simon and Schuster, N.Y. See Durant "Notes" at end of volume.

Hence, it is the local Roman Catholic priest who functions as your mediator to God, not Jesus Christ. Additionally, you may pray to one, or more of the designated saints, or it's statue to intercede for you to Christ on your behalf!

However, there are two aspects of Romanism that flatly contradict the words of Jesus and can in no way be reconciled, or amended to mean otherwise.

1st: Jesus said, *"All authority has been given to me in heaven and on earth"* (Matt. 28:18).

2nd: Jesus said, *"I am the way, and the truth, and the life; no one comes to the Father but through me"* (John 14:6).

The official position of Romanism teaches that the Church stands between the believer and God. That there is no communion between God and the believer as the Church dispenses grace through the **sacraments**.[160] It is the Church that takes care of the believer's relationship to God by means of the Catholic priest who intercedes for you by the power granted him by the Roman Catholic pope, head of the "Holy Roman Catholic Church." Hence,

---

[160] The word "sacrament" is not found in the Greek N.T. The Latin wd. "sacramentum" is derived from the Gk. wd. "mysterion," in English it is "mystery." A mystery generally means a secret disclosed and is now transparent. In the N.T. a mystery is an open secret now revealed in Jesus Christ; He is the mystery of God once concealed, now revealed. See "The Oxford Companion to the Bible", Bruce M. Metzger & Michael D. Coogan, Oxford Un. Press, Inc. 1993.

salvation is exclusively within the confines of the Roman Church.

"Sacerdotalism" as defined above, is diametrically opposed to what Jesus taught about being *"Born Again"* by water and the Spirit (Jn. 3:3-6), and that is the one and only way to enter the kingdom of God. Being born again is a direct operation of God in the life of every believer (Jn. 1:12-13); it is by grace through faith in Jesus Christ that we enter into the kingdom of God and begin to share in His life, to live by His divine life (I Peter 1:4).

But Catholicism teaches that you live by **Sacramentalism** which supersede your need to establish a personal relationship with the Lord by faith. And because "baptism" is administered to infants in the sacramental system (but who cannot confess their faith in Jesus Christ, or repent of sins, etc), they are "consecrated" by religious ceremony that has no correspondents in Scripture.

People then and now, who are ignorant (and or, deprived, [or just spiritually lethargic])[161] of the Scriptures are victimized by the Roman Catholic Church and it's sacramental thinking and become unwitting "Sacrament Worshippers."

Stated plainly, to be a **"Sacramentalist"** means you are completely dependent on the appropriate sacrament

---

[161] During the Middle Ages most of the "Catholic priests" were as ignorant of Scripture as the laity.

being administered to you by the appropriate person to have a relationship with God. The sacraments are priestly ceremonies that confer divine grace and salvation to the recipient by the incantations spoken by the Roman priest. The efficacy of the sacrament is dependent upon the forms and formulas used in the ceremony. Hence, miraculous power is inherent in the ceremonial sacrament, it is not dependent on personal faith or even the moral character of the one who administers it.

Romans 6:6, Ephesians 4:22, Colossians 3:9 all speak of the *"old man"* of sin who willfully and actively engaged in sinful behavior. What infant can lay claim to an old man of sin for which they are repenting in order to be baptized having their sins washed away? And thus, made new in Christ?

Personal participation with God is simply not required under the Sacramental system of the Roman Church. Meaning, it is the prerogative of the "Magisterium"[162] who actually constitute official Church doctrine with the stamp of imprimatur. It is these who constitute this "office" who determine your relationship to God.

Simply put, here's how it looks:

---

[162] The "magisterium" defined, is the living, teaching office of the Church who give authentic interpretation to the word of God, whether written (i.e., Scripture), or from tradition. The magisterium ensures the Church's fidelity to the teaching of the Apostles in matters of faith and morals. See glossary of Catechism of the Catholic Church, 2nd ed. 1992. None of which is found in the word of God.

1) The Roman Model   2) The Biblical Model

God⇨Chruch⇨You   God⇨You⇨Church

The first model is to render obedience to the Roman Church, which stands between you and God.

The second model is to render obedience to Christ, he alone is your mediator between you and the Father.

> ➢ The first requires the intermediary sacramental Roman system.
> ➢ The second requires personal faith in Christ alone.

In the Roman system the Holy Spirit is actually done away with, He is not needed at all because the Church stands between you and God. The Church with all its sacraments stand between you and your Lord, which are administered exclusively by an ordained Roman priest.

Biblically this is the place of the Holy Spirit according to I Corinthians 6:19;

> "Or do you not know that your body is a temple of the Holy Spirit who is in you, whom you have from God, and that you are not your own."

It is the Holy Spirit that intercedes for us unto God our Father as we seek Him out;

> "In the same way the Spirit also helps our weakness; for we do not know how to pray as we

should, but the Spirit Himself intercedes for us with groanings too deep for words; and He who searches the hearts knows what the mind of the Spirit is, because He intercedes for the saints according to the will of God" (Rom. 8:26-27).

It is the impartation of the Holy Spirit from the Lord Jesus to the believer who assists us in seeking and knowing Him and His will;

*"I will ask the Father and He will give you **another** Helper,[163] that He may be with you forever; that is the Spirit of truth...you know Him because He abides in you"* (John 14:16-17).

We have been given ("*another Helper*"), the Holy Spirit by God as a result of our faith in Christ Jesus, and it is He who reveals the Lord Jesus to us in our spirit so that we may be united in Christ to our true Father.

Jesus called the Holy Spirit—"*another Helper*" (John 16:14), a helper like himself, who is also called "*the Spirit of truth*" who leads us into a deeper relationship with the Lord Jesus (vv.5-15).

Our point is this, that there is no place for a "Church," a "pope," a "Sacrament," or a "Magisterium" that dictates conditions, or stands between you and your Lord Jesus in coming to the Father. This relationship is entirely

---

[163] Helper is the Gk. wd. "Paraclete" who "stands beside." He is to be with us in the world, as Christ is with us in heaven. The Holy Spirit, our Helper is one with the Father and the Son.

dependent upon His grace and your personal reception and intentional participation with Him by faith.

So far, we have seen in some detail two of the most misleading and devastating doctrines that have emerged out of the Roman Church;

1. Baptism of infants by sprinkling and without faith
2. The Lord's Supper, via transubstantiation

From here, we will press into another egregious error of the Roman Catholic Church, via, the **Sacraments**.

The Mass

The Roman Catholic "Mass"[164] was developed over long centuries stretching back to before

the time of Christ. Adopted from an amalgamation of ancient Roman religious rituals out of raw paganism and combined with O.T. Jewish ceremonies. The central feature of which is to conjure up the presence of Christ's physical body in the bread and wine, called the "eucharist"—by invoking special words from the Latin and Greek languages.[165]Nevertheless, the performance

---

[164] The performance of the Mass is what creates the holy eucharist, which is the third sacrament of seven in the Roman system.

[165] Although the mass is today commonly delivered in English throughout most of the US.

of the "Mass" is still nothing more than a dead pagan ritual without any biblical basis.

It is in the performance of the "Mass" that Christ is said to be made physically present in the bread and wine through the hands of a consecrated Roman priest and immolated upon the altar-table (immolate is "to slay," or "to kill" the victim as a sacrifice to God).

As previously noted, the Roman Church did not formally adopt the doctrine of the "eucharist" until 1215 AD at the 4th Lateran Council and with it "transubstantiation" as its official dogma,[166] simply because it was still being debated and developed, and that is because it was not fully agreed upon by the ecclesiastical authorities of the Roman Church.

It is important to remember that only an ordained Roman priest can perform the Mass which consecrates the bread and wine into the real body and blood of Jesus Christ, via "transubstantiation." The "lay person" cannot perform this ritual.

Priests, monks, brothers, altar boys, and nuns along with numerous other Catholic orders (i.e., the Knights of Columbus, the Jesuits, Dominicans, Franciscans, Augustinians and many other monastic orders) all find their roots in one or more of the pagan "mystery" religions of ancient Babylon adopted into the Roman empire over its five-hundred-year existence (which

---

[166] Ibid.

began some two-hundred and fifty years prior to Christ), and distilled into the Roman Catholic Church.

Within Rome's pagan clergy and deities were;

- The "pontiffs" (or, priests) who offered ritual sacrifices for Rome.
- The "Flamines" (or, kindlers) who assisted the priests in altar sacrifices.
- The "Salii" (or, Leapers) who performed celebratory dance to ring in the new year.

- The "Fetiales" who sanctified treaties and declarations of war.
- The "Luperci" (or, Brotherhood of the Wolf) performed strange rituals and dances of their own called "Lupercalia."
- The college of "vestal virgins" served the goddess Vesta at the city's hearth, and sprinkled holy water from the sacred fountain of Egeria.
- The Roman goddess "Juno Regina" was hailed as the queen of heaven.[167]

All of these, and many more found their way into the priesthood, convents and canonized saints of the Roman Catholic Church in one form or another. As we continue, we will remind the reader that the national consciousness of ancient Rome was steeped in idolatry and they welcomed these new foreign deities and religions into

---

[167] The month of June is named after Juno Regina.

the pantheon of their indigenous gods, and willingly learned their rituals.

Rome's pagan priests and altar servants made up an elaborate clergy system. Rome's chief priest was called "pontifex maximus" and was elected by the pontifical college.

First: The pontiffs (priests) offered ritual worship to the gods by gifts and sacrifices in order to win their favor or avert their wrath. Only the trained priests who learned the secret mysterious rituals could conduct these highly choreographed ceremonies, while uttering very solemn vows and prayers to the various gods. These became the Roman Catholic priests, and the pope of Rome took the pagan title of the pagan chief priest "pontifex maximus,"[168] followed in descending order by cardinals, bishops and priests.

Second: As religious "orders" began to develop within the structure of the Roman Catholic Church from the early 4th century onward the pagan Flamines, Salii, Fetiales became "altar boys," "monks" and "brothers" within the Roman Catholic system.

Third: The pagan Luperci became organizations like the "Knights of Columbus", and the "Knights Templar", etc, of the Roman Catholic Church.

---

[168] The Roman emperor presided as pontifex maximus (high priest) of the state religions of Rome.

<u>Fourth</u>: The vestal virgins of pagan Rome became the nuns of the Roman Catholic Church. Originally the vestal virgins were young girls ages six to ten who took a vow of virginity and served for thirty years. After which they could return to public life, but few ever did.

<u>Fifth</u>: Juno Regina, the Roman queen of heaven was transferred to Mary the mother of Jesus as the queen of heaven. The Roman Juno Regina was a picture of motherhood, and sexual activity. Whereas, Mary was a chased virgin who never had sexual relations with her one and only husband, not before or after the birth of Jesus, but remained a perpetual virgin, which is contrary to the narrative of Scripture.[169]

From these ancient orders came the organization and hierarchical structure of the Roman Catholic Church that continued the religious rituals of pagan Rome with the same disease of Babylon entwined within the warp and woof of the Fallen Church.[170]

Mystery Religions

The mystery of the Roman Mass is, and always has been an unrevealed mystery, precisely because it has been taken from the origins of paganism, the mystery religions of the ancient near east such as Babylon. Contrary to the

---

[169] See, Matt 13:54-56 (Ps. 69:8); Mk. 3:31-35; Jn. 7:3-5, for the siblings of Jesus. We leave it to the reader to decide from the Scriptural accounts whether Jesus had brothers and sisters born of his mother Mary, wife of Joseph.

[170] All of the Reformers of the Middle Ages referred to the Roman Church as the "Fallen Church" and without exception to the popes as the Antichrist.

New Testament writings a mystery is an open secret, something that is revealed in Jesus Christ. Yet to this very day, no one in the Roman Church can explain how "transubstantiation" occurs in the sacrifice of Jesus on the altar in the course of the Mass, except to say, "it is a mystery."

This does not fit with the words of Jesus in the Gospels, or of Luke in the Acts, or of the Apostle Paul in I Corinthians. The Lord's supper is nowhere else spoken of in the N.T. writings, with the possible exception of Jude v.12, where we read of the *"love feasts"* which many interpreters take as a reference to the Lord's supper. There is also a reference in Revelation 19:9, to *"the marriage supper of the Lamb..."*, but which encompasses a celestial banquet and not the supper of the Lord as presently observed on earth.

The supper is spoken of in the N.T. as eating in *remembrance*, and that we look forward to the Lord's return in so doing (Lk. 22:18-19; I Cor. 11:25-26). That is the mystery revealed

from the O.T. Passover supper in the N.T. Lord's supper—he, namely Christ Jesus, is the Passover Lamb just as Paul stated it; *"For Christ our Passover has also been sacrificed. Therefore, let us celebrate the feast..."* (I Cor. 5:7-8).

Transubstantiation is truly a mystery within the Roman Church because it is so very contradictory; **first**, from a biblical understanding, and **second**, from a practical experience.

1. There is not a single reference to a Sacramental Mass by Jesus or the apostles.
2. There is no communal aspect to the eucharistic transubstantiation Mass.[171]

As we have shown, its origins are from the pagan mystery religions of Chaldea, Babylon, Egypt, etc, imported into Rome as it rose to became a world power.

In those ancient pagan religions, a mystery was a guarded secret by the religious specialist initiated into its rites and ceremonies dedicated to its gods. These priestly specialists were sworn to an oath never to reveal the secret religious rites disclosed to them least a curse come upon them, such as they agreed to when they took the solemn oath upon entering their priesthood or order. This in fact, is the point of the tonsured haircut of various orders of monks and priests, and the conspicuous white collar worn by the Roman priest—these serve as a reminder of the oath of secrecy they have taken and the curse that awaits them if they reveal their secret rites of initiation.

Beyond the oath of secrecy, the Romanist takes upon entering his or her order, which is based on: **First**—a private knowledge; And, **Second**—on the repeated performance of the religious rite.

Concerning the repeated performance of the Mass, the priest is said to be reenacting the brutal death of Jesus

---

[171] It is performed exclusively by one man; the ordained Roman priest, no one else's presence matters.

on the cross of Golgotha. And in the course of this ritual ceremony the priest calls Christ out of the eternal realm of heaven, who is enthroned at the Father's right hand, and puts him into the wafer-host, via "transubstantiation"—which becomes a wafer-god, which is why they can bow down to it, worship it, and be encouraged to gaze adoringly upon it: It is god! [172]

What Roman Catholic would deny this?

This is the same Satanic influence that fell upon the children of Israel coming out of Egypt when they first engaged in idolatry and made for themselves a god in the image of a golden calf to whom they bowed down and worshiped and offered sacrifice! [173]

The paganism of the Roman Mass correlates exactly to the pagan mystery religions of ancient Egypt and Babylon, etc. And the Catholic priests who are deceived by this so-called secret knowledge and the accompanying rites and ceremonies become more and more connected to the ritual performance of the Mass and end up buying into the deception that they actually possess the mysterious power to conger up the very body and blood

---

[172] The Catholic may wish to have "god" capitalized. But how, seeing that it is nothing more than bread.

[173] See, Exodus 32 on the worship of the golden calf. See also, Ex. 20:2-6, the first of the Ten Commandments which strictly prohibits the making of an idol to worship (no matter who's image it supposedly bears).

of Christ in the Sacramental ceremony of the Mass and stuff him into the wafer-host.[174]

The influences of the Greco-Roman mystery religions and rites filtered into the Roman Catholic Church at the hands of many semi-converted pagan philosophers who became influential teachers in the church, and then moved into positions of appointed authority, and eventually into the Roman priesthood. The result; a hierarchical, top-down authoritarian structure that mirrored that of the Roman empire.

Because the Roman Church is a Sacramental system that teaches you only receive *"justification"* from sin by the administration of the Sacraments, they unwittingly relegated personal faith in Christ completely unnecessary. For that matter, evangelism is unnecessary. The first Sacrament, of which is baptism, is administered to the infant in the Roman Church. But even within the Roman Catholic Church infant baptism was not consistently practiced until the mid-5th century. In fact, infant baptism did not gain wide spread acceptance until after 400 AD, primarily due to the influential writings of Augustine,[175] and because of his belief of

---

[174] See, II Thessalonians 2:7-12, particularly v.11 and how this fits the Roman sacramental system.

[175] Even though Augustine wrote much that appealed to non-Sacramentalists, and non-Roman Catholics –at heart Augustine was still a Sacramentalist and very much Roman Catholic.

"inherited sin"[176] which necessitated the baptism of infants.

Concerning the topic of infant baptism, we invite you to read Philip Schaff's "History of the Church"[177] who surveys the first three centuries' writers on baptism (including during the time of Constantine), and shows that adult baptism was the normal practice and that discipling, or teaching preceded baptizing everyone only after their confession of faith in Jesus Christ, following the example of Acts 2:37-38.

As it stands, Romanism teaches that every Mass is a (re)sacrifice of Jesus Christ every bit as much as the very crucifixion on Golgotha in 30 AD, and that through the administration of the Sacrament in the eucharist you receive salvation regardless of any other thing going on in your life.

That is, you may be an overt practicing sexual pervert, a murderer, or any other kind of active criminal sinner, it does not matter the sin you are engaged in, simply eating the consecrated wafer-host placed on your tongue imparts anew salvation to the recipient.

---

[176] Some refer to this as "original sin" which came from Adam and Eve. I.e., every human being inherits their sin, although Ezekiel 18 overtly declares the sins of the fathers are not inherited by their children.

[177] See, Bible.org/question/history-origins-of-infant-baptism. See also, "The Church of Rome at the Bar of History", William Webster, 2019, who sites many church writers of the first 3-centuries.

In short, the entire Sacramental system of the Roman Catholic Church is a demonically influenced counterfeit of the true and genuine ekklesia that Christ Jesus planted and upon which his apostles continued to build, he being the Chief cornerstone (Eph. 2:10-22).

No wonder virtually all the reformers during the "Age of Reformation" considered the Roman Church to be what Revelation 17:5 says;

> "BABYLON THE GREAT, THE MOTHER OF HARLOTS AND OF THE ABOMINATIONS OF THE EARTH."

As we close our study, I would like to leave you with a description of "Brainwashing"[178] with a couple of modifications;

> *"Brainwashing is best accomplished when you have no idea that it is being done but simply occurs as part of the fabric of your life. While you may "feel" that something is wrong, you are being programmed nonetheless. Think about the stories you're told, the Mass you attend, the rote level prayers and Creeds you are taught, with these facts in mind."*

This is not only a good description, but a good definition of how brainwashing occurs. It's how Communists become

---

[178] The description of brainwashing is from U.S. Senator John N. Kennedy of Louisiana. Specifically, the last half of the last sentence was modified.

Communists, how liberals become liberals, how legalists become legalists, how institutional Christians become institutionalized, and how Catholics become Catholics. It is *"the fabric of your life."*

They are consistently involved in a lifestyle saturated in the movement they are a part of, its teachers, its teachings, its schools, it's worship and being a part of the entire structural makeup without question.

They virtually live in an echo chamber of the same words, same thoughts, same behaviors, surrounded by propaganda, lies and half-truths that when confronted with the actual, genuine truth they are left with limited options:

One—simple denial and continue to live in self-delusion.

Two—try in vain to answer the obvious objections to their misplaced beliefs.

Three—honestly examine the Scriptural evidence and compare it to the internal evidence of their own spiritual senses that cry out for *"spirit and truth."*

Only when this third option is embarked upon with abandon will anyone be brought into an experience of Jesus Christ where he is allowed to be Lord of your life, and master of your soul; mind, will and emotions.

Anything short of this is not Christianity.

The Religious Veil of Noise

One last matter we must all face regardless of our particular persuasion, or stripe of "Christianity" is that of *faith*. Defined as the assurance and conviction of things not seen except through spiritual eyes so as to see the unseen (Heb. 11:1, et., al.). It is to believe that you stand in the presence of the Lord, unmoved by any other consideration. Yet not in an external way as if to evaluate yourself by your performance. But in an internal way, to behold the glory of the Lord as in a mirror looking back at you, being transformed into His image, as Paul spoke of in II Corinthians 3.[179]

It is here and only here that the inner religious veil of noise is taken away so that we may see the Lord as standing in His very presence. This is where real and genuine self-evaluation takes place, because it is in our inner man, within our spirit that the Lord makes Himself known and it is there that He makes His habitation.

For many, faith means there must be an outward doing of some ministry by which he measures himself before the Lord. Weather teaching, preaching, converting the lost, correcting and establishing the saved, going to church, attending worship services, a music ministry, and all sorts of things that go with it. In general, they are constantly engaged in some type of ministry or good deeds. We are not speaking of that sort of faith.

---

[179] See, II Cor. 3:15-18, and 4:3-4.

To be blunt, no good deed, no ministry, no matter how "Christian" it may appear, if it does not spring from an inner faith it is of absolutely no value in the Lord.

The Christian who seeks God externally pursues the path of reason and logic and gives a great deal of attention to his thoughts, and feelings, and the deeds he engages in, these are matters of great importance to them, and they do not go unnoticed.

Both the externally spiritual Christian as well as the internally spiritual Christian know the virtue of suffering, of being fervent in love, are skilled orators and expositors of the word, and the former speaks of these matters often and engages in them at every opportunity. In fact, they are hard to ignore. In this way they seek notoriety among the brethren and believe that they find greater acceptability with God, a closeness with God by their "doing, thinking, and feeling"—that others just don't share.

That is what they project and it is largely how they are seen by others.

In this state they are so preoccupied by outward religious performance that they cannot see through the veil of religious noise. They remain in the crowded Courtyard of sacrifice and blood, and are forever contemplating the altar and the washing in the laver, the more sacrifice, the more washing. Yet never enter through the veil into the quietness of the Tent of Meeting for deeper intimate fellowship with the Lord. There to bask in the light of Jesus Christ, inhale His sweet fragrance, and gathered around His table to behold His beauty in the silence of simple fellowship with Him and with other brothers and sisters.

Is there are any clearer picture of this than between the two sister, Mary and Martha, from Luke 10:38-42. Mary took the quiet posture of a disciple, and gave her full attention to Jesus. Martha however, took the position of active-outward ministry in serving, but was given no attention or credit for this at all. So, she spoke up and complained to the Lord, who gently reminded her of such unnecessary worldly worries and business. Only one thing was necessary, and Mary had chosen it; she gave her love and attention exclusively to the Lord and he, in return, basked in her love. Jesus had found in her God's Most Holy dwelling place hidden within her spirit.[180]

The Silence of Simple Worship

This form of worship is almost entirely lost to this generation, to this century of Christians in America and Europe. The loss began to creep into American society in the late 1930's and continues to this very day, and will continue into the foreseeable future.

Kinetic war seems almost inevitable between the US and China (and other countries), if so, it will disrupt the entire order of the world, and the luxuries of all

---

[180] Part 2 of that story between the two sisters may be read of in John 11 and 12:1-11, where they are at peace and in harmony with one another and the Lord.

Americans will be dramatically interrupted and the world will be thrown into utter chaos from top to bottom.

When social and economic commerce begins to grind to a halt perhaps then we will revert back to a form of silent worship. When we will sit quietly before the Lord Jesus and simply behold him and wait. Our economic pursuits will be concentrated of the basic necessities of food, shelter, and clothing. And perhaps then we will revert back to simple family meals at home around the dining room table.

Already there are people who are returning to this form of worship. They see that the biblical from of home worship is actually the form God has modeled for us, not just in the Old Testament but also the New.

When God spoke to Moses about building a tabernacle it was for the purpose that He might *"dwell among them"* (Ex.25:8). All of Israel, tribe-by-tribe, family-by-family then encircled the tabernacle each in his own home tent facing the dwelling of God in His tent in the very center of the encampment. This pattern continued once in the Promise Land only on a larger scale; the mobile tabernacle was replaced by the permanent temple in Jerusalem and all Israel encircled it throughout the land.

In both cases God's habitat was central to Israel. When we come to see the centrality of Christ in our individual and collective lives, apart from the modern Church system, and can gather together around Him from *"house to house"* (Acts 2:42b), we will have learned the meaning of worshiping in *"spirit and truth"* (Jn. 4:23-24).

The expression of any church come-together is Jesus Christ. When He is central an expression of love for Him will be evident in a spontaneous out pouring of praise to Him, and that love and affection will spill over one to another.

The simplicity of worship in spirit and truth is undistracted by worldly systems and the contemporary models of Church in an endless pursuit of a perfect worship service. It does not exist, yet there is a continual expectation of it.

True worship seeks only Christ, and He is inexhaustible.

We will close with the words spoken by the angel to John when he was caught up into heavens and shown the Revelation of Jesus Christ. Here, the apostle seems to have been overcome by the overwhelming grandeur of his surroundings and lost track of his senses and bowed in worship to the angelic messenger, not once, but twice! And the angel reprimanded him for this, we read;

> "Then I fell at his feet to worship him. But he said to me, 'Do not do that; I am a fellow servant of yours and your brethren who hold the testimony of Jesus; worship God. For the testimony of Jesus is the spirit of prophecy'"(Rev. 19:10).

Again, in Revelation 22:8-9 we read;

> "I, John, am the one who heard and saw these things. And when I heard and saw, I fell down to

worship at the feet of the angel who showed me these things. But he said to me, 'Do not do that. I am a fellow servant of yours and of your brethren the prophets and of those who heed the words of this book. Worship God.'"

"Worship God"—it simply cannot be stated any simpler or more direct than that.

Revelation 3:20, "Behold I stand at the door and knock; If anyone hears My voice and opens the door, I will come in to him and will dine with him, and he with Me."

Made in the USA
Monee, IL
31 August 2023

0ce83c7c-f161-404f-ade2-cf1c356abb5fR01